FANDOM ACTS OF KINDNESS

A Heroic Guide to Activism, Advocacy, and Doing Chaotic Good

TANYA COOK AND **KAELA JOSEPH**

Smart Pop Books
An Imprint of BenBella Books, Inc.
Dallas, TX

Smart Pop is an imprint of BenBella Books, Inc.
10440 N. Central Expressway
Suite 800
Dallas, TX 75231
smartpopbooks.com | benbellabooks.com
Send feedback to feedback@benbellabooks.com

BenBella and *Smart Pop* are federally registered trademarks.

Printed in the United States of America
10 9 8 7 6 5 4 3 2 1

Library of Congress Control Number: 2022026553
ISBN 9781637741702 (trade paperback)
ISBN 9781637741719 (electronic)

Copyediting by Lydia Choi
Proofreading by Isabelle Rubio and Michael Fedison
Text design and composition by Aaron Edmiston
Cover design by Brigid Pearson
Printed by Lake Book Manufacturing

Special discounts for bulk sales are available.
Please contact bulkorders@benbellabooks.com.

In memory of Holli and Sarah,
you were exactly what this book is about.

To all the fans who fight for good; you're our heroes.

CONTENTS

FOREWORD

"Look, I'm simpler than you think. I've figured one thing out about this world – just one, pretty much. You find a cause, and you serve it. Give yourself over, and it orders your life."
—Meg, *Supernatural* episode 7.21, "Reading Is Fundamental"

We are wired for community, we survive by connection, we thrive when we feel like a contributing part of something larger than us. These are beliefs that order my life and why I connect so strongly with this book.

Fandom at its best can be a source of wellbeing and healing for many of us as individuals and, I also believe, for the world at large. Like any power, though, it must be wielded correctly and navigated intentionally, and this book has many helpful pointers to guide you in whatever way serves you best.

When harnessed correctly, we in fandom can be an unbeatable positive force. A group of people brought together by a shared ability to imagine fantastic worlds into being (often much better than the one we are experiencing), many of us seeking community in this new realm because we have had the great empathy-building experience in past spaces of being othered, sometimes brutally. We are a unique band of individuals, most of whom have already experienced living life outside the boundaries of the status quo, and therefore are not afraid to cast aside outmoded systems for new, more promising possibilities.

As someone who has spent over a decade attending fandom conventions, as an actor in a fantasy TV show, and, for the past six years, as executive director of a 100% volunteer nonprofit born out of fandom, I live and breathe fandom as a force for good.

From my experience, fandom and volunteering can be a wonderful fit. In order to choose to be a volunteer, to put time and energy into creating a more supportive world for no monetary gain, one has to have certain qualities, qualities that those in fandom often have in abundance:

1. A vivid imagination, because we attempt to achieve things many deem impossible.
2. A capacity for joy and hope, because we truly run on morale alone much of the time.
3. A sense of responsibility to team, because we only get through this together; trying to go it alone so rarely, if ever, works.
4. A willingness to break with and question assumed "rules" of the game (for example, that we humans are motivated solely by money or that selfish gain alone determines our productivity) because "being the change" requires us to be willing to, well, um . . . change.

If you are picking this book up, I hope it works as a useful guide to help you make the most of your fandom experience. Having spent years in this world, I found the map Tanya and Kaela so deftly put together to be a truly comprehensive overview with which to navigate through it all in a healthy and fulfilling way.

May your journey be a truly inspiring one!

Rachel Miner
Executive Director
Random Acts
August 2022

INTRODUCTION

*L*ong ago, oracles foretold a group of Chosen, called Nerds or Geeks, Shippers[1], or sometimes just Fans, who would embark on an epic journey to save the world. Through trial and tribulation, they would fight for the underdog, stand up for justice, find the courage to speak truth, and challenge the powers that be. Their enthusiastic, weird, chaotic kindness would spark revolutions. Though their world was dark and full of terrors, the Chosen found that fighting the good fight was both tenable and transformative. Instead of waiting to be saved, they became the heroes they needed. They learned that their real superpowers were imagination, compassion, and the social networks they tapped into along the way!

As nice as epic origin stories can be, the truth is you don't have to be a chosen one or some mythical hero alluded to in an ancient prophecy to make a difference. You don't need supernatural powers or abilities. You already have the power to change the world for the better. Yes, you, Dear Reader! And you don't have to

---

1   By shippers, we refer to fans who, at least partially, define their participation in fandom as being associated with relationships between characters, canonical or fan-created.

1

hike through troll-infested mountains to do it. All you have to do is gather your kindness, compassion, and curiosity and read this book. It will be more fun than marching through Mordor, and you can totally take breaks for Second Breakfast and Elevenses. Promise.

This book was written to help fans like you tap into their power to do good in the world. Our own quest started as an intellectual investigation into fandom-based charity work but quickly grew into a much larger campaign. Over six years, we developed expertise in participatory fandom, fan culture, and fandoms as social movements by researching fandom-based activism. This included interviewing fans, attending conventions and events, and using our backgrounds in social science to better understand how fans are making a difference. We also participated in our own share of fandom-based activism. Throughout our research, we learned about a multitude of inspiring ways fans were using their love of pop culture to engage in social movements, and when we presented our research directly to fans at conventions, the question we were asked most often was, "That's great, but how do I get involved—how do I *actually do* fan activism?" This book answers that important question.

Let's start at the very beginning—a very good place to start. When you read, you begin with A, B, C; when you . . . learn how to make the world a better place with fan activism, you begin with . . . definitions. Okay, so that didn't rhyme, but we had to give a shout-out to Tanya's *Sound of Music* fandom at least once!

Let's unpack the term "fan activism." What is meant by "fan," and what is meant by "activism"?

Fans are folks who identify as supporters of a specific sports team, celebrity, or performer or who are enthusiastic consumers of specific kinds of popular culture. This book focuses on fans of popular culture media products, including (but not limited to!) fans of television shows, video games, books, and movies. Of course, the word "fan" can also be a verb in English. And while we're not using the word "fan" to mean "moving air currents" or "spreading out," in this context, being a fan also implies action and interaction with other fans. Being a fan is not just something you are; it's something you do. Many of us, as fans, don't just *watch* our favorite show—we *live* it. We make fan art, write fan fiction, attend conventions, and seek out prized photo ops and autos from our favorite actors and writers.

Now that we share an understanding of who a fan is, let's turn to "activism." Activism is a key component of how societies change. Activism is direct action taken by a group of people to either bring about or prevent change. In the 1960s, Civil Rights Movement activists worked to fight legal discrimination against Black Americans. Not only did they succeed in changing our laws with the passage of the Civil Rights Act of 1964, but they also forever changed American history and culture. Activism can look like the March on Washington in 1963, led by Dr. Martin Luther King Jr., and it can also look like college students in the 1990s holding sit-ins to protest their universities' contracts with corporations who manufactured licensed products in sweatshops.

So, what is "fan activism"? It's the actions that fans take to contribute to the good of their communities and make the world a better place. Fan activism can be anything from a fan running a geeky 5K for charity to joining a protest march in support of undocumented immigrants. The main thing that distinguishes fan activism from other kinds of activism is that fans use their identities as fans and their connections through fandom to get things done. Sometimes those connections are the bonds formed between fans themselves. Sometimes those connections are the ones formed through parasocial relationships with celebrities who have a unique sociopolitical reach due to their public platforms. When we discuss parasocial relationships throughout this book, it is important to remember that "parasocial" means "sort of social": not as close of a personal bond as what we may have with friends, family, or partners. Rather, it is a social relationship built on our being a fan of someone or a thing that someone is a part of. When we discuss parasocial relationships, we mean to use those relationships within an appropriate context. This context both acknowledges how these relationships are structured differently than other social relationships and is respectful of a celebrity's space and privacy.

Fan activism can look a lot like social movement activism—actions focused on attaining social, political, or cultural change in the name of the greater good. Fandom-based activism can also look like civic participation, volunteerism, and charity work. Although many scholars of social movements would not consider these last examples to be part of activism, they're included here because they have deep personal and political meaning for fans.

Engaging in activism through fandom is more common than you might think. Martin Luther King Jr. even engaged in fan activism! In the 1960s, during a gathering of the National Association for the Advancement of Colored People (NAACP), King met with Nichelle Nichols, who played Nyota Uhura on *Star Trek*. Nichols was, at the time, planning to leave the show. However, King, a fan of the series, saw how the Civil Rights Movement could be influenced by *Star Trek*'s fandom. He is quoted by Nichols as saying,

> *Don't you realize how important your presence, your character is? . . . Don't you see? This is not a Black role, and this is not a female role. You have the first non-stereotypical role on television, male or female. You have broken ground . . . For the*

first time, the world sees us as we should be seen, as equals, as intelligent people—as we should be.[2]

Fast-forward several decades, and *Star Trek* is still influencing activist leaders. Stacey Abrams, best known for her voting rights activism, has cited her love of the show as an influence when working through real-life problems. The fan-turned-politician even cameoed on *Star Trek: Discovery* as president of United Earth.

Throughout this book you'll find numerous examples of fan activism and inspiring real-world and fictional connections. The book is designed to be read from cover to cover, but each chapter can also be read on its own. You can work through the activities included over and over and return to the resources you create whenever needed. That's right: we're teachers, and we gave you homework. But don't worry—it's fun homework!

Our mission is to help you turn your passion into work for good. We, as fans ourselves, believe in the power of fandom to save the world. From helping you home in on what causes are most important to you, to building your fellowship of like-minded nerds, we've got you covered. We'll help you get ready for your journey by sharing inspiring stories and examples of fan activism. You'll also learn how acting in line with your values and building community help you level up your self-actualization stats.

Did you know that fans of the '90s TV series *Xena: Warrior Princess* have donated over $28 million to charity? How about the *Supernatural* fans who helped rescue over three hundred people from flooding after devastating hurricanes in 2017? What about the *Star Wars* and *Star Trek* cosplayers who put aside their "which

---

2   Arielle Kass, "A conversation with MLK Jr. kept Nichelle Nichols from exiting Star Trek," *Atlanta Journal-Constitution*, February 26, 2021, https://www.ajc.com/news/atlanta-news/a-conversation-with-mlk-jr-kept-nichelle-nichols-from-exiting-star-trek/X3Z7Q7LGN5BSVMVUFTDN3O63RU/.

is better" debates to visit sick kids in the hospital? Speaking of *Star Trek*, this book wouldn't exist without the organized efforts of passionate, mostly female, fans who saved the original series from cancellation. (Shout-out to the amazing Bjo Trimble!) All of these are uplifting examples of how fans have worked for the greater good. Many of us are inspired by stories of heroism, and now, with this book, you can go beyond inspiration to action!

While the goal of this book is to help you do some good throughout your time on this rock floating through space that we call Earth, we also want you to have fun along the way. That's what makes fan activism so powerful, after all. You are making the world better through something you love. So, activists assemble; boldly go; get on the road; jump to lightspeed; come on, grab your friends; and set off on this adventure in fandom acts of kindness!

Chapter 1

START WITH WHAT YOU LOVE

"That's how we're gonna win. Not fighting what we hate; saving what we love."
Rose Tico, *Star Wars: The Last Jedi*

Have you ever found yourself buried in a book you couldn't put down? Told yourself that you're going to watch *just one more* episode (okay, maybe two more . . . make that three) of your favorite show? Maybe you've spent hours or days trying to create the perfect work of fan art, fan fiction, or epic cosplay. You may have even found yourself passionately trying to convince your loved ones to read/watch/play something you've found that lights up your world so they can share in your sheer and utter joy.

Well, my friend, we have good news and bad news. The good news is, you're in love. The bad news is, like all things that thrive on and cultivate emotional intensity—a new relationship, a new project, a new puppy—you may be looking at some sleepless nights ahead of you. The great news is that if you identified with any of this, you probably know that falling fast and hard into a fandom is totally, 100 percent, turn-the-dial-to-eleven worth it. That big, energetic, head-over-heels love is also the thing that will get you started on your path to fan activism. It is the first resource you need on your journey, the first part in building your very own Arc Reactor to help channel your passion into action, just like how Tony Stark found the key to clean, renewable, sustainable energy through his love of science.

Now, Tony didn't just intuit how to build something as fantastical as an Arc Reactor, nor was his shifting of the mission of Stark Industries from weapons manufacturing to clean energy production and technology innovations done without self-examination. The man loved science, and that love helped fuel his evolution from billionaire playboy philanthropist to Iron Man. But he also needed to understand what he wanted to build *before* he could build it. He explored his values and shifted his company's mission from making weapons to making green power. He didn't just love science; he wanted to see science save lives, not destroy them, and the Arc Reactor was one of many ways he was able to live that value.

In order to dive into your own work as a fan activist, you'll also need to identify your values, as well as learn how to enact those values. You'll need to be able to differentiate between using your values to help you find out what you love, and using your values to help you find out the best way to express that love through action. We'll lay out a road map to help you find your passion, identify your values, and then align the two. Consider the skills you already have and are looking to build. Think about what values guide your actions. Finally, complete a fun alignment worksheet to help you identify your values!

IDENTIFYING WHAT YOU LOVE

In figuring out what you want to do, it helps to focus on at least one specific cause you intend to fight for. This doesn't mean you can't champion multiple causes; most causes intersect in some way. Picking a cause just gives you a focal point around which to ground your work.

Consider the fandoms you love the most. What particular story is the most powerful for you? What about that fictional world or those characters inspire you? When you start to identify with the characters in a particular story or the structure of a particular world, you may unconsciously start comparing yourself to them. Once you become aware of this, you might notice that the characters you love share some of your values. Characters you love to hate or worlds with extreme injustice could function as a sort of anti-reference group or cautionary tale.

When you think about all of the problems in the world, it can feel overwhelming and impossible to know what to focus on. It's important to consider what causes or projects speak to you most directly before deciding where to act. Is there a particular social identity that you want to explore, and do you want to help others who share that identity? Does your community or city need specific kinds of activism or social services that are not currently being provided? Do you have time, money, skills, or other resources to donate? For example, we are passionate about transgender rights and volunteer with organizations working to further justice for gender-diverse folks. In the past, Tanya volunteered as an after-school tutor with the Boys & Girls Club. As a former latchkey kid, she wanted to draw on her love of *Star Wars* and Marvel to connect with and help other kids in similar situations who needed a positive relationship with an adult. Kaela volunteered as an HIV test counselor because they had grown up in communities with limited access to sex-positive health resources. Kaela's love of sci-fi and horror shows helped them translate health information in fun, accessible ways by connecting difficult-to-understand medical concepts to relatable tropes in popular television series.

CAUSES

Below are some examples of causes. "Cause," in this context, refers to a pressing issue, social problem, or need that is currently unmet. Circle your top three and rank them in the order that they feel most important to you today (it's okay if the order changes in the future). Feel free to write in any causes you do not see in the list below. This is by no means a comprehensive list.

Animal Rights	Anti-Bullying	Child Welfare	Clean Drinking Water
Disability Rights	Education Access	Environmentalism	Gender Equity
Homelessness	Hunger / Food Scarcity	Immigration Rights	Indigenous Rights
Intimate Partner Violence	LGBTQIA+ Rights	Mental Health	Natural Disaster Relief
Physical Health	Prison Reform	Public Health	Racial Equity / Anti-Racism
Sexual Assault Awareness	Suicide Prevention	Veteran Services	Workers' Rights

1. _____

2. _____

3. _____

VALUES

Now let's think about how to align your values with your causes. First, we need to discuss what values actually are. Values are more than just *what* is important to you. Values are about how you want to show up for the things that are important to you: who you want to be as an activist. Values are broadly defined as moral beliefs; they can be both comprehensive ideologies and abstract ideas. Your values are shaped by the society, culture, and individual context in which you were raised. They may differ from person to person based on your race and ethnic group identification, political ideology, country of origin, or personal experiences.

Values are also different from goals. A goal can be achieved, whereas a value is something you are always striving for—a sort of moral compass, if you will. One does not simply walk into Mordor to destroy the One Ring, for example. It ultimately takes the path forged by the value of friendship to get the Ring to Mount Doom. Once they achieved their goal of destroying the Ring, however, Samwise and Frodo didn't just stop working on their shared value of friendship. There was no scroll back in the Shire on which they could check off "friendship" as fully achieved. They would presumably continue to forge new paths together as the environment around them changed and new adventures came and went.

It's possible to have the same set of values as someone else but to define those values differently. For example, the central characters in Marvel's *Captain America: Civil War* value heroism and human life, but the Avengers split into two opposing groups because the behaviors they associate with those values are wildly different. Each character has a goal of saving humanity, but their different interpretations of the values of heroism and human life lead them down different paths. And we, the audience, are essentially asked to choose which side we would follow, knowing that neither is inherently right or wrong—both are just different interpretations of the same thing. Those different interpretations matter, however. In the anime and manga *Death Note*, central characters Light Yagami and L both proclaim, above all else, to value justice, even going so far as to describe themselves *as* justice, but their interpretations of the value vary dramatically. Light sees justice as achieved through the mass murder of criminals and the ensuing fear in the public to avoid crime, no matter the cost. L, on the other hand, sees justice as adherence to the law and seeks to put an end to the murders committed by Light via the Death Note. Justice is usually thought of as a noble value, but *Death Note* asks us to question what that value really means and what makes the pursuit of it noble or not. Similarly, many of the so-called villains in *Batman* comics, shows, and movies hold values we typically deem admirable, such as environmentalism (Poison Ivy and Ra's al Ghul) and marital love (Mr. Freeze). We deem these characters villains, however, because of the unethical and deviant behavior they engage in. This is to say that you don't just need to identify *what* your values are, but also *how* you intend to live them in a way that aligns with doing good.

Identifying your values can be like building a character in a role-playing game (RPG). While some aspects of character building can be specific to gameplay, such as armor class in *Dungeons & Dragons*, other aspects, such as moral alignment, determine how a character will go about achieving their goals in a given campaign. Here's an exercise, based on some common characteristics of RPG character sheets, to help you start identifying your values.

VALUES: WHAT CHARACTER ARE YOU?

ALIGNMENT

Associated Values: Morality and Agency

This describes one's relationship to morality (good, neutral, evil) and social systems (lawful, neutral, chaotic). If you're familiar with this way of describing alignment, use the space below to describe your own. If you aren't familiar with this, or aren't sure exactly what your alignment would be, use the space below to describe how you would most like to be in relation to social governances such as laws, religious/spiritual rules, etc. If you are using the traditional alignment structure, keep in mind that all alignments have strengths—just because you want to *do* good doesn't necessarily mean you have to describe your alignment as good. Circle the characters or alignments you associate with, and then write your own alignment in the space below. For reference, we've paired the traditional alignments in *D&D* with some *Game of Thrones* and *Batman* characters to illustrate the positions.

_____

_____

_____

_____

_____

CHARACTER ALIGNMENT CHART

Lawful Good (Crusader):	Neutral Good (Benefactor):	Chaotic Good (Rebel):
Follows order and structure; committed to good	Committed to altruism over structure	Committed to individual freedom/equality over structure; would sacrifice self for others
Character Examples: Ned Stark, Commissioner Gordon	**Character Examples:** Samwell Tarly, Alfred Pennyworth	**Character Examples:** Daenerys Targaryen (at least for the first seven seasons!), Batman
Lawful Neutral (Judge):	**True Neutral (Undecided):**	**Chaotic Neutral (Free Spirit):**
Prioritizes law and order (structure) over morality	Prioritizes own needs and self-interest over morality or structure; may also work to maintain status quo	Rejects authority but is more self-interested than chaotic good
Character Examples: Stannis Baratheon, Harvey Dent	**Character Examples:** Bronn, Catwoman	**Character Examples:** Olenna Tyrel, Poison Ivy
Lawful Evil (Dominator):	**Neutral Evil (Malefactor):**	**Chaotic Evil (Destroyer, Demonic):**
Committed to evil but also to structure; think authoritarianism or dictator; will obey laws or change laws to their advantage	Similar to a sociopath—will hurt others to accomplish their self-interested goals	Wants to break down the world or destroy order and implement chaos; could also be preoccupied with revenge
Character Examples: Tywin Lannister, Ra's al Ghul	**Character Examples:** Roose Bolton, the Penguin	**Character Examples:** Joffrey Baratheon, the Joker

RACE, CLASS, AND LANGUAGES

Associated Value: Culture

These aspects describe a character's ancestral backgrounds as well as other cultures they may have immersed themselves in. Use this section to describe important cultural practices you engage in or aspire to engage in more, such as religious and ethnic norms, family traditions, etc.

_____

_____

_____

_____

_____

Bonds

Associated Value: Relationships

This refers to the people a character is closest to or cares most about. Use this section to describe what relationships are most important to you and how you most want to show up for others. What kind of child, guardian, sibling, partner, friend, etc. do you want to be?

_____

_____

_____

_____

_____

PERSONALITY TRAITS

Associated Value: Interests/Hobbies

This typically refers to a character's unique likes and dislikes, usually influenced in some way by other personal characteristics, such as abilities. Use this section to describe what interests make you uniquely you and how you most want to participate in those interests. For example, as part of a fandom, you might make fan art, write fan fiction, attend cons, etc. Feel free to include non-fandom-related interests here as well. For example, you may have an interest in reading that drives you to form book clubs or donate books to local charities when you finish them.

_____

_____

_____

_____

_____

The great thing about values is that we can have lots of them, and they can shift over time as we learn and grow. The values that are most important to you at the start of your activist work may therefore change based on the experiences you have or the people you come to know. Just like your favorite characters, you aren't just changing the world; the world is also changing you!

THE IMPORTANCE OF FLEXIBILITY

Living your values means being flexible, like Elastigirl (or Elastiboy, or Elastiperson). You don't need to have super-stretching abilities, but you do need to be able to stretch your values around new situations. In *Incredibles 2*, Elastigirl (aka Helen Parr) is faced with a values conflict: she values both her family and the law. When Helen says, "To help my family, I gotta leave it; to fix the law, I gotta break it," she recognizes the conflict and adapts her behavior to meet her values. She does this again when her understanding of the context in which she is practicing her values changes. She flexes and adapts. It is likely that, at some point, you, too, will be faced with a values conflict. You might come to understand your cause differently as you engage more in activist work. You might experience a life-altering event that changes your perspective on your cause, your fandom, or life in general. You might even have a falling-out with your fandom, or at least with certain aspects of it. What's important is that you flex instead of flee, and figure out how to make the most of the new information you have.

If you write or read fan fiction, think of flexibility like recontextualizing characters in an AU (alternate universe) fic (fan fiction story). When we read AU fic, we accept that though the characters are like the ones we know from whatever original work the fanfic is based on, there are critical aspects of the AU that change their life trajectories and therefore certain aspects of their values and actions as well. For example, the characters in an AU fic where Neville Longbottom, not Harry Potter, is the Chosen One may still have similar values to those of the original characters we know, but they may go about expressing those values in a different way based on their different experiences. If you're reading an AU fic where Neville and Harry are both tax accountants who meet in a broken elevator on the twentieth story of a London skyscraper, those values would probably be even further changed. Think of the shifts in your life and activism as if you're entering an AU where you now have new information that informs your character build. You can revisit this chapter and its character build activity to see how your fan activism has changed over time—and how *you* have changed over time. We can't all be Elastigirl, but flexibility and reflexivity (understanding and thinking about what you're doing and why you're doing it) is crucial for effective activism.

Now that you've identified what you love and the causes and values that are important to you, it's time to take the next step on your hero's journey—to look beyond the *what* to the *why*.

Chapter 2

KNOW YOUR WHY

"I don't want to kill anyone. I don't like bullies. I don't care where they're from."
Steve Rogers, *Captain America: The First Avenger*

Steve Rogers knew why he was a hero. He even volunteered for the job, just like you are doing by reading this book! But he wasn't a hero because he took the Super Soldier serum. In fact, we see in several instances throughout the Marvel Cinematic Universe (MCU) that the serum itself corrupts. No, Steve is a hero because he knows himself—he knows who he cares for, the importance of his relationships, and his place in his community and society at large. Let's consider another Steve, the title character from Cartoon Network's *Steven Universe*. Like Rogers, Steven Universe is a hero defined by compassion, but unlike Rogers (at least in the MCU), we get to see a lot of Steven's inner monologue and, over time, the development of *why* his heroism works. Steven's compassion ultimately makes him the hero of his own story, but that compassion is fought for and won through a complex interplay between himself as an individual, other humans and extraterrestrial Gems, his communities in Beach City and the Gem Homeworld, the Little Homeschool institution he runs, and the larger societies of Earth and space. Steven is able to bring together war-torn factions and diametrically opposed species, as well as ultimately preserve the universe at large, because the show makes room for the complex interplay between these different layers of being—different layers that all have a part to play in social change. The series starts with Steven saving others and ends with them saving Steven. He betters society, and, in turn, society betters him.

Steve Rogers knew he could "do this all day"—"this" being to fight or do anything else to do what was right—because he knew the ultimate benefits of his actions. Similarly, Steven Universe knew he could heal and be healed because he understood that everyone has a purpose in the world, despite their imperfections—that, "if every porkchop were perfect, we wouldn't have hot dogs," and thus, everyone is worth saving. Knowing your "why" can keep you motivated when things get tough. Let's look at why fan activism matters and all the ways doing fan activism benefits you as an individual, your community, and the world!

EXAMPLES OF FAN ACTIVISM TO INSPIRE YOU

FANS AND ORGANIZATIONS HELPING INDIVIDUALS

Xenites, fans of the television series *Xena: Warrior Princess* (1995–2001), are one of the most generous fandoms around and a great example of how fan activism and engagement benefit local groups, communities, and the world. Like other fandoms, Xenites coalesced around a show they found inspiring and created a community through interactions online and at conventions. Inspired by Xena's path toward redemption and service, fans were motivated to fundraise at conventions and online, all in the name of the "greater good.³" Since the show first aired, Xenites have raised millions for international organizations, including Greenpeace and the Starship Foundation, an organization that supports pediatric health in New Zealand. In addition to contributing to organizations, this small group of passionate Xena fans has directly donated thousands of dollars to its own community members who find themselves in need of financial assistance. For example, when a longtime fan and community member needed help with unexpected home renovations in 2020, her Xenite family raised over $5,000 to cover the repairs in just a few days. Given that *Xena* has been off the air for over twenty years, the efforts and commitment of the Xenite community are even more impressive.

Similarly, fans of the sci-fi program *Wynonna Earp* created a social media hashtag—#EarperSupport—for fans struggling with health or financial issues, or who just needed some emotional support. In our research, we've seen fans start GoFundMes and other campaigns for one another many times, and many have successfully raised tens of thousands of dollars.

Financial assistance is not the only way fans have helped one another. *Supernatural* fan Geff Gruber was only twenty-six when he learned he would eventually need a kidney replacement due to a rare disorder. Thanks to his sister's social media savvy, Gruber got the attention of the *Supernatural* fandom through a themed GoFundMe page. But things really took off when Stands, an online store, took note of it. Stands regularly partners with actors, mostly in the *Supernatural* fandom, to sell themed merchandise, with a portion of the proceeds benefiting a charity or cause close to the actor's heart. Stands retweeted the GoFundMe link and

---

3   "The Greater Good" is the title of episode 21 in Season 1 of *Xena: Warrior Princess*.

raised over $9,000 by promising to mail merchandise rewards to those who donated at least $20. *Supernatural* actors Misha Collins and Jared Padalecki also shared the link, and another fan, Lauren Angelini, noticed. Angelini got tested to see if she was a match for donation and flew to New York to donate her kidney in early 2021. Many fans we spoke with talked about how fandom has saved their lives, but when Gruber said, "*Supernatural* saved my life," he meant it literally.[4]

Even more amazing is that Gruber is not the only fan to receive a lifesaving kidney donation through the power of fandom networks. In 2009, Jeff Romanoff received a kidney from another member of the *Star Wars* charity cosplay group the 501st Legion, Eric Seemann.[5] On the anniversary of the transplant in 2021, Romanoff talked about how Seemann's donation saved his life and motivated him to raise money and awareness for others with kidney issues via his Twitch streaming channel. Like Gruber, however, Romanoff also acknowledges the importance of *Star Wars* and the fandom in literally saving him: "The movies saved my life, in a sense, because I got hooked up with so many great people and so many friends that somebody stepped up to the plate . . . I hope my story energizes people into doing the right thing, and maybe changing somebody else's life."

While these stories are amazing, fans also help support one another every day. As a community, fans interact regularly with one another. Social media can be both a blessing and a curse in

---

4   For more on Gruber and Angelini's story, check out: Andrew Garcia, "A 'Supernatural' kidney donation: Bellmore man finds kidney donor with celebrity help," *LI Herald*, April 8, 2021, https://www.liherald.com/merrick /stories/a-supernatural-kidney-donation,131567.

5   For more on Romanoff's story, check out: "A Force for Good," National Kidney Foundation, May 3, 2021, https://www.kidney.org/newsletter/ force-good.

this respect. In a world where we are increasingly less socially integrated with our neighbors, fan communities can serve to provide options for friendship, entertainment, and connection. Sharing messages of encouragement or even fan art can create bonds between fans. Like any social group, fandoms can foster friendships that last decades. When you think about what makes someone a friend—sharing interests and hobbies, caring about that person's overall happiness, spending time together, and supporting one another—can you apply those touchstones to any of your fandom community members? In 2020, during the initial weeks of the COVID-19 pandemic, fan groups hosted online games, viewing parties, and even virtual conventions to help alleviate the boredom and pain of social isolation. Of course, not all fandom relationships or friendships last, and not all of them are positive. For more on the dark side of fandom and how to protect yourself, see chapter eight.

FANS ENGAGING IN COMMUNITY SUPPORT

Each year on August 3, people around the world celebrate Esther Day, a Nerdfighteria fandom holiday created to honor the memory of Esther Earl. Esther Earl, a young vlogger and fan of *Harry Potter* and Vlogbrothers, passed away in 2010 at age sixteen from aggressive thyroid cancer. Inspired by Esther's energy and compassion, John Green partially based the main character in his best-selling YA novel, *The Fault in Our Stars*, on Esther. In her honor, each year on Esther's birthday people around the world tell their friends and family that they love them. Esther's family also founded a nonprofit organization, This Star Won't Go Out, that supports families facing childhood cancer. This Star Won't Go Out has raised over $450,000 since its founding in 2011 to support families experiencing financial hardships associated with treating childhood cancer. Most of this fundraising is coordinated by young people around the world through bake sales, art projects, carnivals, and other events. More than ten years after Esther's passing, fans are still finding Esther's videos online and joining the fight to support families.

In the aftermath of the devastating hurricane season of 2017, *Supernatural* fans from around the world worked together to coordinate rescuing people in the southern United States who had been stranded in their homes by floods. Brandy, a self-identified fan of the television series and all things horror, succinctly expressed this relationship between personal fulfillment, volunteerism, and building community while describing the organization of Supernatural Rescue (SPN Rescue) immediately following the aftermath of Hurricane Harvey in 2017:

> *Sometimes I can't wrap my head around it . . . I don't think they [the rescue coordinating organization] expected that we were willing to spend fourteen hours solid doing something for nothing, for little return other than our own self-satisfaction.*

Brandy and other SPN Rescue volunteers described how they became friends by working together and chatting via Slack. Years later, many still interact regularly and have come to think of themselves as a community. At one point during the hurricane season of 2017 and the height of volunteering, an estimated 30 percent of online volunteers were *Supernatural* fans. Clearly, the experience of working together helped to meet the individual need to feel connected and efficacious while also benefiting the broader community. Fans literally saved lives!

Years later, these fan helpers have formed a distributed global network that provides social integration for those who participate and can be used to help others. Helping in the aftermath of a disaster makes individuals feel like they are acting in line with their values and brings people together to form strong community bonds. Fan activism is similar in that it helps both individuals and groups and cements the bridging capital built through action.

FANDOM GOES WORLDWIDE FOR CHANGE

One of the most effective and far-reaching examples of fan activism is GISH, or the Greatest International Scavenger Hunt (formerly known as GISHWHES—the Greatest International Scavenger Hunt the World Has Ever Seen). Started by actor Misha Collins (*Supernatural*) in 2011 as a way to engage with fans on Twitter, GISH has evolved into a weeklong annual scavenger hunt, typically taking place the first week of August. Gishers (people who participate in GISH) organize into teams of ten to fifteen and work to complete a list of hundreds of items, document their work, and then upload the evidence (photos and videos) as proof of their completion. Each item is worth a number of points; items range from the charitable and kind (taking pastries to your local fire department or donating to food pantries) to the weird and seemingly impossible (getting an object with your team's name on it into orbit). The team with the most points at the end of the hunt wins an all-expenses-paid vacation to a spectacular destination. Collins joins for part of the trip. In the past, winners have visited New Zealand, Iceland, and Laos.

The magic of GISH is not just its additive effect, however. The donation items and acts of kindness do add up and certainly make a difference, but what's incredibly impressive is how GISH uses the power of social networks to fundraise hundreds of thousands of dollars for specific causes in a matter of days. And they do this every year! By incentivizing teams to seek donations from individuals not on their team for the "Change a Life" item, Gishers harness the exponential power of social networks—or, as sociologist Mark Granovetter describes it, "the strength of weak ties."

Who you know matters; people in your network can connect you to other networks. What starts as a single action in a game can have far-reaching positive effects, and the beneficiaries may not know that fans' love of a deadpan, literally-minded, awkward angel made all the difference! In recent years, GISH has encouraged registration (registration typically costs between $20–$25, but assistance is available if this is cost prohibitive) by donating a portion of registration fees to charities. In this way, Gishers have ensured the preservation of over forty thousand acres of rain forest, removed thousands of unexploded land mines in Laos, and sent thousands of dollars to True Colors United, an organization that supports homeless LGBTQIA+ youth. For the "Change a Life" item, Gishers typically raise $200,000 by getting ten people to donate at least ten dollars. In 2021, the fundraising supported a non-politically affiliated, free children's hospital in Afghanistan that specializes in treating kids who have suffered wounds from gunshots and explosive devices.

Wait a minute, you might be thinking. *These GISH examples just sound like coordinating donations and charitable giving.* And you'd be right—they absolutely are. But by making charitable work and volunteerism fun, social, and engaging, GISH helps people identify what's important to them, sustains participation, and leverages the underutilized resource of fan passion. Also, in 2020, GISH shifted the hunt and its items to support more direct activism. The hunt included several panels about racism and racial injustice in the United States and encouraged participants to learn about and donate to Black Lives Matter organizations and write letters to protest wrongful imprisonment and incarceration.

BREAKING DOWN CHANGE INTO ITS PARTS

At least as far back as Aristotle, scholars have argued that express-ing concern for others and engaging in social activity to help others is not only a fundamental human behavior but also a nec-essary one. It is how humans as a species survive and thrive, from the fictional Fremen on Arrakis in *Dune* who share the limited water of their land and from their bodies, to real-life communi-ties wrecked by natural disaster sharing labor in order to rebuild. Coming together in the wake of disaster is an underlying narra-tive in many fantasy and sci-fi adventures because it is so central to our human existence. The Fellowship of the Ring is formed out of a collective need to rid the world of the potential of Sauron's will. In *Game of Thrones*, the houses of the North join to conserve their resources against the threat of the White Walkers and the impending harsh winter. The survivors of Caprica and the col-onies in *Battlestar Galactica* come together to sustain humanity until they can find a new home. Helping one another is Human-ity 101. Simply put, the reason we need activism is because we are human. To understand this human need, it helps to understand how social change occurs.

Social change isn't linear. Change happens at various levels or within intersecting elements of influence, simultaneously. It's "a big ball of wibbly-wobbly, timey-wimey stuff,"[6] akin to the swoops and swivels of the Jeremy Bearimy timeline in *The Good Place*. We can't fully separate elements of influence from another, but we can consider how change in each element impacts the whole. One way to conceptualize social change in this way is

---

6   The Tenth Doctor describes time as non-linear or a "big ball of wibbly-wobbly, timey-wimey stuff," in Doctor Who Series 3, episode 10, which originally aired June 9, 2007.

by using something called a Social-Ecological Model of Health. Organizations like the US Centers for Disease Control and Prevention (CDC) use this model to depict the interwoven relationships between various elements of socio-ecological influences on public health concerns, such as violence prevention. The model recognizes that individual needs and differences are just some of many factors impacting social change when considering public health interventions, with the other factors including interpersonal relationships, community, organizational culture (if an organization is involved), and society at large. While the model has not been applied specifically to activism, it makes sense to draw this parallel. After all, activist causes, like public health initiatives, are about ensuring public good, and both share the same interlocking levels of influence that must be addressed to promote effective change.

Using the social-ecological model as a template, we can picture the path to social change as being like the rainbow Bifrost between the realms in Asgard—interlocking elements of influence that form a bridge between worlds—the one we are living in, and the one we hope to create through activism. In other words, you can't change yourself without affecting your community and vice versa. In this metaphor, fan activism is like Heimdall's sword—when used effectively, it can command cosmic forces to bring together these various elements of influence needed for change.

Color in the graphic on the following page to make your own rainbow bridge! Start with red for Element 1 and then continue with orange, yellow, green, blue, and purple. You can even use this as a bit of self-care as you think through how you'd fill in the elements.

6. Society at Large

5. Organizations and Institutions

4. Parasocial Relationships

3. Fandom Communities

2. Close Interpersonal
Relationships in Fandom
and Activism

1. Individual
Participation
In Fandom
and Activism

ELEMENT 1: INDIVIDUAL PARTICIPATION IN FANDOM AND ACTIVISM

Recent research in psychology supports the notion that activism is beneficial to the individual in its own right.[7] In other words, volunteerism and activism can be intrinsically motivating for individuals—we engage in them because it makes us feel better to help others. Sociologist Émile Durkheim theorized that being disconnected from society was not only bad for communities but also detrimental to individuals. When people feel alienated from social groups, they may experience "anomie," or feeling apathetic and detached from others. This feeling of isolation, detachment, confusion, or contradiction between norms and values can lead to social problems such as crime, drug use, and suicide. Think of Squidward in *SpongeBob SquarePants* or the Queen of Hearts in Tim Burton's *Alice in Wonderland*. Feeling out of place and alone in society, Squidward becomes disillusioned and depressed, while the Queen of Hearts becomes an unpredictable tyrant. Humans, even those who are introverts, have a basic need to feel as though they are integrated into communities and making a difference. All of this to say that individual participation in fandom and activism is fulfilling because it connects us to others, and our connection to others is important to our own well-being. This is especially important in the wake of a natural disaster. When individuals are unable to help, or when they perceive the disaster as human-made or something done to them (an oil spill or municipal water being contaminated with lead, for example), rather than an act of nature (a tornado or storm), they experience alienation that can lead to social isolation, increased self-harming behavior, and weaker community bonds. An individual-level effort toward

---

7   For more on this point, see: Malte Klar and Tim Kasser, "Some benefits of being an activist: Measuring activism and its role in psychological well-being," *Political Psychology* 30, no. 5 (2009): 755–77.

social change or disaster relief can be as simple as changing a behavior that contributes to pollution or donating five dollars to a cause you care about, and it goes a long way.

Think about your own participation in fandom and/or activism to date. What makes you feel good about embarking on this kind of work? What are the ways your individual participation in fandom might be turned into activism? In what ways have the types of fan activism you have witnessed or read about impacted you on a personal level, the same way that your favorite book, game, show, movie, etc. might also have impacted you in deeply personal ways? Use the space below to write about examples of activism that are inspiring to you, and/or brainstorm about how your fandom participation might morph into activism:

ELEMENT 2: CLOSE INTERPERSONAL RELATIONSHIPS IN FANDOM AND ACTIVISM

Within a given fandom, you probably have some friends you are closer to than others. You might also share your fandom with members of your family or with friends you were close to before you were ever involved in the fandom. The close interpersonal relationships we have shape how we approach both fandom and activist work. These are the people who reinforce our values and challenge us to grow. They step up and support us when burnout arises. Think about the initially lone(ish) wolf, Holden, in *The Expanse*. His individual participation in his society is clear—he is a former naval officer whose goal is to keep flying and to avoid getting tangled up in Earth, Mars, or Belter politics. It is his ties to Belters Detective Miller and Naomi Nagata, plus the close bonds he forms with his crew, however, that eventually set him back on a path toward a greater good and position the crew of the *Rocinante* as vitally important to saving the universe. Our personal relationships can reinforce our activism. We can use them as motivation and positive reinforcement.

Consider who your close, personal crew is. Who is going to help you keep the *Roci* flying when Mars, Earth, or Marco Inaros is on your tail? Who is going to assure you that your ship—and you—are going to be able to hold it together? It's okay if you don't have a crew yet! Many people gravitate to fandom as a subculture because they don't feel fully connected elsewhere, so fandoms are ideal places to recruit a crew. Think Spike, Jet, Faye, Ed, and Ein coming together aboard the spaceship *Bebop* in *Cowboy Bebop*. Anyone can find a crew, even if it is a motley one. In fact, it is sometimes that shared interest and shared existence in the margins of society that fuels activism. We want the rest of society to be as welcoming and affirming as our fandom communities are. Use the space below to write down the members of your crew. Include a few potential crewmates you might recruit or some ideas about where to find them:

_____

_____

_____

ELEMENT 3: FANDOM COMMUNITIES

Fandom communities can be formal, informal, and everything in between. They can be as small as a weekly *D&D* group or book club, as large as the over one hundred thousand fans who attend San Diego Comic-Con every year, or as formidable as the millions of audience members who flock to theaters on opening night. Defining the parameters of your community will help you engage in fan activism by helping you understand who your biggest allies are in a given fandom and what the reach of your community is. For example, the small *D&D* group could band together to donate everything in their collective cabinets to a local food pantry or community fridge, while a fandom of thousands could fund a community fridge, and a fandom of millions could work to dismantle the very systems of poverty that make community fridges a necessity in the first place. You might find your community in online forums; at conventions; or at a protest holding up signs with General Leia's face plastered across it, demanding women's rights—the possibilities are endless, and they can change over time as you get more involved.

After the last official Creation Entertainment Xena convention in 2015, which had been held annually in Burbank, California, a fan named Penny Cavanaugh started the Xenite Retreat. The retreat runs for a long weekend at a campground in California north of LA and is best described as an adult summer camp for Xenites, complete with softball games, activities, and group meals. Most importantly, the retreat continues the tradition of the charity breakfast originally started at the conventions, where Xena merchandise and collectables are auctioned off, with the proceeds donated to charity. Attendees of the Xenite Retreat contributed over $50,000 to charity in just four years. Penny and the organizers of the Xenite Retreat relied on the established community of the fandom to build and sustain activism.

When she volunteered as tribute, Katniss Everdeen didn't intend to spark a revolution. But the "girl on fire" did just that when she united the hearts and minds of people throughout the oppressed districts of Panem. Katniss's heroic turn would have ended with winning the games had she not managed to build alliances between diverse communities. As a member of District 12, Katniss and her friends and family knew hardship and deprivation. In the face of that, they built the resource that was available to them—community—and used that to support their very survival. But Katniss also needed the skills and support of Cinna, Effie Trinket, and even Caesar Flickerman in the entertainment communities to help her gain attention and visibility. Katniss's compassion and bravery even brought other oppressed districts to their cause—no mean feat, given the lack of resources and communication between districts.

List some groups and communities you are already a part of or interested in joining in the space below:

_____

_____

_____

_____

_____

ELEMENT 4: PARASOCIAL RELATIONSHIPS

Parasocial relationships are the affiliations you have with celebrities and other creatives who are involved in the making of the thing you fan over. These relationships matter to fan activism because celebrities usually have a bigger reach than we do as fans, meaning they can get more people involved in a cause than we can. Think about our previous example—Katniss Everdeen in the *Hunger Games* franchise. While every individual in the districts who rises up against oppression is important in the eventual social change that ensues, Katniss is able to use her celebrity (albeit reluctantly, in her case) to both bring about rebellion and ensure that the people's cause is not lost to the individual interests of President Coin. While celebrities do hold power, it is important to remember that the relationship in this model is cyclical; we impact them, and they impact us, and we all impact social change.

An excellent example of the power of parasocial relationships is the campaign launched by Lady Gaga related to the repeal of the now rescinded Don't Ask, Don't Tell (DADT) law, which prevented lesbian, gay, and bisexual service members from serving openly in the US military. As Dr. Lucy Bennett, cofounder of the Fan Studies Network, discussed in a 2013 blog post about the subject,[8] though Lady Gaga is a self-described queer woman, she has not served in the military, and we have no reason to believe that she intended to back in 2010 when she posted a video showing her followers how to contact their representatives and request that they vote to repeal the DADT law. While we can't know for sure, it's likely

---

8   For more information, see: Lucy Bennett, "Examining Celebrity Activism and Social Media: Lady Gaga, Fandom, and Don't Ask, Don't Tell," *RE.FRAMING ACTIVISM* (blog), May 13, 2013, https://reframe.sussex.ac.uk/ activistmedia/2013/05/examining-celebrity-activism-and-social-media-lady -gaga-fandom-and-dont-ask-dont-tell/.

that the issue was instead somehow brought to Gaga's attention. Gaga's social media post about repealing the ban then inspired fans Lauren and Ellie to start making their own videos. They not only called their senator but also filmed themselves going around their college dorm asking others to do the same. Their efforts were eventually rewarded when that senator responded via YouTube that he had received their messages, thanked them, and then in fact voted to repeal. The DADT repeal was made effective in September 2011, and while Lady Gaga and her Monsters (the name of her fandom) are by no means solely or even mostly responsible, there was clearly at least some cyclical impact. Gaga impacted fans, who impacted a senator's vote, which impacted the repeal, and Gaga saw that she and her fandom could make a difference and continues to speak out on social issues.

Think about celebrities who inspire you with how they use their public platforms. Do you follow celebrities who, like Lady Gaga, share information about actions you can take to influence social change? What issues and causes are they concerned about or sharing information about? Is it possible to connect with other fans of that celebrity to organize donations? Of course, we don't want to engage in inappropriate or spamming-type behavior with celebrities and their social media platforms. But curating your social media feed and looking at what kinds of issues celebrities are lending their voices to can help you connect with other like-minded fans and learn how to "brand" your causes to accomplish goals. Use the space below to list some celebrities or public figures who inspire you:

_____

_____

_____

ELEMENT 5: ORGANIZATIONS AND INSTITUTIONS

Organizations are a specific group with a shared goal, while institutions are more bound by law or custom. A political party is an organization, while the government is an institution. Creation Entertainment and Fan Expo HQ, for example, are organizations that host the fandom institutions that are fan conventions. Both organizations and institutions rely on individual and community support in order to function. If you want to bring down an organization or institution that isn't serving the people, your best bet is to show the people that the organization or institution isn't serving them and to encourage them to stop participating. Chapter six goes into more detail about economic strategies for doing this, but what is important here is the interplay between all the circles through which social change occurs. Sports fans, for example, have been known to buy back stadiums, and the teams that play there, to influence the equity of the fan/sport relationship. Legion M, a fan-owned entertainment company, has been involved in the production of films like the *Jay & Silent Bob Reboot*, *Mandy*, *Tolkien*, and *Colossal*. Legion M capitalizes on the relationship between fans, communities, organizations, and institutions. It aims to make use of equity investment legislation to ensure that fans have the opportunity to invest in the kinds of content they would like to see (while also being transparent about the inherent risk of investment). Legion M also relies on fan/celebrity relationships to increase fan engagement so that it can fund projects celebrities are already attached to. It's activism in that it seeks to diversify film and the investment landscape via a "by fans, for fans" model of production, and it really exemplifies the layering of these different circles of the social-ecological model.

Use the space below to write down some organizations you are a part of, or some you want to join, and some institutions you support:

_____

_____

_____

_____

_____

ELEMENT 6: SOCIETY AT LARGE

We use myths to communicate to one another about how to maintain safety and order, and when to rise up. Myths like "the boy who cried wolf," for example, are intended to teach children the importance of truthfulness and respecting rules. Other myths, like stories around Robin Hood, inspire us to challenge social order that is corrupt. As stories that are told to explain natural or social phenomenon or teach lessons, myths are as essential to who we are as humans as our desire to help one another is. Change the myth, and you change humanity. And because fandoms form around myth—the myth of a person's public persona, or the literal myths of stories told through visual art, music, television, film, sports, etc.—fan activism is, in a way, the ultimate act of activism. When organizations like the 501st Legion, the Mandalorian Mercs, and the Rebel Legion engage in fundraising and other charitable acts, they aren't just engaging in fan activism; they are living the myths that the *Star Wars* franchises reinforce: anyone can be a force for good.

Unfortunately, the reason we need myths and their messages, like "good always triumphs over evil," is because there will likely always be some sort of foe, concrete or existential, that threatens humanity. Activism isn't really about changing society irrevocably or without need for improvement in the future—it's about moving the needle on the dial of our collective narrative just a little, away from the dark side and toward the light side. So be warned: if you take down the one or two Death Stars, you can't be either complacent or surprised if and when the New Order forms in the vacuum of power left behind by the Empire. Just as the diagram of social change is cyclical and interlocking, the process of action needs to be ongoing. Don't give up! There are close personal allies, whole fandom communities, public figures, and organizations and institutions standing alongside you in this work. Just don't keep them, like Force ghosts, on the outskirts of your Endorian tree house celebration. Let them be with you. Always.

Use the space below to consider what broad social changes you think would make the world better:

_____

_____

_____

_____

_____

_____

_____

_____

CONNECTING THE ELEMENTS

Let's work our way through the prompts you just completed with a real-world example to show how the elements of influence are aligned in fan activism.

A passionate advocate for sex worker rights and self-identified geek, Pasha reached out to Tanya to seek advice on how to create awareness of sex trafficking at fan events like Comic-Con. Pasha and Tanya knew each other because of their individual participation in fandoms and their joint interactions within fandom communities—Elements 1 (individual participation), 2 (interpersonal relationships), and 3 (fandom communities). Tanya suggested creating and hosting a panel about how sex workers are portrayed in sci-fi and fantasy shows can act as a way to attract an audience to spread anti-trafficking and pro–sex worker sentiment. Pasha has since presented at several conventions.

When the largest comic book store in the United States, Mile High Comics, announced it would host a family-friendly, all-ages drag show, protesters threatened to shut down the event. Pasha knew the owner of Mile High and quickly put together a plan to make it a safe and fun event for anyone who wanted to attend. She and Parasol Patrol cofounder Eli Bazan organized a group of volunteers to physically shield the kids entering or participating in the event with colorful umbrellas (parasols) from the anti-LGBTQIA+ protesters. Volunteers from that event have since shielded participants and families at a variety of drag events and story times. Pasha was able to network with prominent leaders (Element 4: celebrity relationships) of national LGBTQIA+ organizations to bolster her own organization (Element 5: groups and organizations). Pasha's experience with activism and her immersion in fandom culture helped her to recognize a broader social need (Element 6) and take action to support LGBTQIA+ youth, their families, and drag performance spaces. Parasol Patrol, now a recognized nonprofit organization, is a great example of how the social-ecological model can help us understand fan activism's ripple effects.

Now look back at what you wrote in previous parts of this chapter. Use the space on the next page to work through your own potential example of how the Elements might align for you. It might help to reverse engineer aligning your Elements here. Element 6: What is a broader social change you would like to see or an issue that needs work? Maybe look back to your values responses in chapter one. Element 5: What organizations are you part of that might be able to help with this issue? If you are not part of any, what organizations are currently working on this issue that could be potential resources? Element 4: Do you know any prominent activists, celebrities, or leaders who are working on this issue? What are they saying about it? What has worked for them and what has not in terms of their messaging? Element 3: What fandom communities are you a part of? Do any ideals and values expressed in the fandom match up with the social change needed? Element 2: Who do you know or have personal relationships with who might be interested in working on this issue? Finally, Element 1: What examples of fan activism do you currently find rewarding or inspiring? How do you want to participate in fan activism?

GETTING BACK TO "WHY"

So why participate in fan activism? Because it's good for you, it's good for your community, and it's good for the world. And it's fun!

1. Individual Participation in Fandom and Activism

2. Close Interpersonal Relationships in Fandom and Activism

3. Fandom Communities

4. Parasocial Relationships

5. Organizations and Institutions

6. Society at Large

Chapter 3

THIS IS THE WAY

"Remember . . . magic is Chaos, Art and Science. It is a curse, a blessing and progress. It all depends on who uses magic, how they use it, and to what purpose. And magic is everywhere. All around us. Easily accessible."
Yennefer, *Blood of Elves*

Learning how something works or how to perform a particular action is usually a pretty important step in any new endeavor. For example, if you've ever played an RPG, tabletop, or video game, you probably had to either read the instruction manual or be instructed about the game's inner workings by a trusted friend or Dungeon Master to figure out what to do. So, how does fan activism work? What are the tools of the game, and how do you use them? And just like in any good RPG, the tools you have access to are dependent on the in-universe gameplay, meaning that the rules of activism will change a little depending on your fandom and cause. This means you need to gain some experience points—that is, you'll need to understand how to play on your own before you play with others and go on advanced quests. Otherwise, the dragons and demogorgons will eat you alive! For example, you'd want to gain experience points in *The Witcher 3: Wild Hunt* through solo tasks, like winning games of GWENT, before trying to assemble a team for the Battle of Kaer Morhen. This is also the way toward effective activism: start small before going big. Your journey as a fan activist will hopefully be a lifelong one, so getting to know yourself, and reflecting on how you want to do this activism thing, is key to making your fan activism journey healthy, fun, sustainable, and efficacious.

GAINING EXPERIENCE POINTS THROUGH RESEARCH

Starting small can mean just learning more about a cause. As a fan, you probably already have some experience with research, as part of fan behavior involves learning a whole lot about a very specific thing. For example, Tanya can quote some episodes of *Star Trek: The Next Generation* for you verbatim, and Kaela can talk your ear off about all the queer coding in animated Disney films. Learning about your cause is simply cultivating experience points, which can then be used to level up for activist quests.

Start your individual research journey by curating a social media news feed or resource list. Identify what issues are important to you and take a few minutes every day to learn something about them. Find a couple of news sources you trust to present as unbiased reporting as possible, and subscribe to their email updates or follow their social media outlets. Websites like Snopes.com, PolitiFact.com, and Factcheck.org can be used to fact-check any news, statements by politicians, or viral stories you are unsure about. Check out local news sources for your city, state, region, country, etc., as they tend to cover the kinds of issues that are going to be most relevant to you and your communities.

Some news sources, like Vox, are explanatory in nature, meaning they try to avoid bias and simply explain what something is. Outlets like this also typically share their sources, creating a level of transparency about any bias that does come through. Some causes have their own news outlets, such as *PinkNews*, which is popular for information related to LGBTQIA+ stories, or *Ebony*, popular for information pertaining to stories impacting Black communities. You can also set Google alerts for issues you want to keep tabs on.

When deciding how you are going to acquire information, think about what ways news and other information are most digestible for you. Are you a visual learner who needs pictures or videos to accompany new information? Are you an auditory learner who benefits from people talking about a topic? Maybe you are someone who learns best by reading, or kinesthetically by writing about a subject or performing a related action. Knowing how you best absorb new information can help you pick news outlets and other resources that you will be most likely to keep up with. If you aren't sure of your learning style, think about the lessons you enjoyed most in school. What elements of learning did they apply from the above? At the end of the day, the best news and information sources for you aren't just the ones that are balanced; they are the platforms you will keep referring back to, ones that are accessible and that sustain your attention.

It's also important to consider what times of the day or what days of the week are most conducive for learning about issues. For example, many sleep experts recommend avoiding the news (and screens in general!) before bedtime. Consider what times of the day may work best for you and create the least amount of stress. If you work more on some days of the week than on others, it's a good idea to not schedule additional emotionally and intellectually draining tasks on top of that.

Often-overlooked sources of information include your local, state, and national elected officials. Look up your representatives and subscribe to their newsletters, follow them on social media, and attend their town hall meetings. Similar resources exist in other places around the world, especially in places where leaders are elected, and can usually be easily found via your favorite web search engine. Subscribing to resources like these will help you learn about initiatives and issues that directly affect you and your community, which may not be covered in state or national news media sources. Partisanship will, of course, color the ways in which news and other information is shared, but you can always corroborate what you read in these resources by looking up additional sources. Looking at multiple sources helps to avoid the kind of idealistic echo chamber that can result from consuming too few sources on a particular cause.

Obsessively checking the news and other resources, however, can be detrimental to your overall health, so be careful how much you consume. It's especially easy to get into the habit of doomscrolling on social media instead of researching, in which you aren't really engaging with content so much as getting sucked into repeated headlines about disastrous-sounding things. Doomscrolling isn't just bad for your mental health; it can contribute to the spread of misinformation by causing you to retain only the worst parts of a story without much context. Practice setting boundaries to protect yourself by scheduling hours for or enforcing time limits on what you're looking at online. Many devices help you set boundaries by giving you summaries of your screen time or by allowing you to set timers to deactivate certain device settings. You can also note what kinds of sources might be more triggering than others and adjust your consumption accordingly. For example, crisis lines like Trans Lifeline and the Trevor Project share news on social media, but they are attentive to mental health needs and frame posts accordingly, along with the inclusion of how to contact the crisis line if you need support.

Keep track of what you're reading by writing down sources and brief notes about what you read here:

_____

_____

_____

_____

_____

_____

_____

_____

If you prefer to research on the go, you can also jot down notes in phone applications like the Notes app on a smartphone or in a Google Drive document during your commute.

Once you have created a resource that informs you about what is going on in the world, commit to educating yourself about social justice and the movements related to specific issues you care about. Some of us have been fortunate to experience social justice training and education through school or work. However, if you are completely new to issues of social justice, check out the suggested free educational resources list in the Resources section at the back of the book. Even if you are a Jedi Master at social justice or know a great deal about the issue you're working on, it helps to keep learning. If nothing else, it will help you stay connected to others and to current perspectives on the topic. It can be challenging, but it's also a good idea for activists to understand the perspectives counter to your own. This isn't to suggest that you fall into a hate group's social media feed or anything like that! Instead, find a trusted academic or journalistic source and try to understand what the arguments against your cause are so that you are best prepared to frame your issue and respond to them. Think of this like knowing other *D&D* characters' strengths, Constitution scores, spells, etc. You could also think of it like Defense Against the Dark Arts training. It helps all of us to channel our inner wizard and learn as much as we can.

LEVELING UP THROUGH INDIVIDUAL QUESTS

Once you know more about what is going on, you can start going on individual side quests. In RPGs, side quests can build toward a larger, main quest, and individual acts of activism are no different—they can build toward larger goals of collective action.

SIGNING PETITIONS

One of the easiest and fastest ways to get involved is to sign petitions. Many fan communities circulate these online. There are several online sites that allow users to create petitions. Change.org is perhaps the best known, and it is useful for signing and keeping an eye on petitions; however, it is a for-profit company that does not have to disclose how its funds are collected or allocated, and proceeds earned through petitions do not typically go to the petition creators. Instead of clicking the "chip in" option on Change. org, consider donating directly to nonprofits, organizations, or individuals. Another large online social network is Care2.com, founded to connect activists and nonprofits around the world.

Although Care2 partners with and helps to fund thousands of nonprofits, it, too, is a for-profit organization.

Keep in mind that there can be flooding issues with petitions. Flooding is when multiple petitions about the same issue are being circulated and the information redundancy causes us to react as though they are spam—and ignore them. And though petitions alone do not typically create change, they do demonstrate public interest as part of a larger change-based campaign. With petitions so easy to sign and follow, there are just too many for all or even most to be successful, or for them to even get in front of the right people. That said, it also doesn't really hurt to sign some, given how low-stakes the effort is.

EMAILING OR CALLING YOUR REPRESENTATIVES

Technically, when you do this, you are a lobbyist. And though lobbying can, for good reasons, have a negative connotation, all it really means is trying to legally influence a politician or representative to act in your interests. In a representative democracy, you, as a voter, have every right to ask your representative to act on your behalf, so you should feel empowered to contact them. Everyday citizens may not have as much money as huge corporate lobbying groups, but we are the reason these folks have jobs. And, at the end of the day, they work for us!

Use this space to list the contact information for someone you'd like to contact in order to advocate for change:

Name: _____

Email: _____

Address: _____

Phone Number: _____

Social Media Handles: _____

_____

_____

_____

_____

To hear from their constituents, most elected officials hold some form of semiannual or periodic town hall meetings, which are great places to use your voice. Many nonprofit and advocacy organizations will have scripts for you to read or mail to your representative if you are unsure about what to communicate. Use this space to jot down some questions you may have for them:

_____

_____

_____

_____

_____

UTILIZE PUBLIC FORUMS FOR POLICY CHANGE

Many government-funded entities, such as public boards and public health administrations, hold town halls, listening sessions, and other forums for public/consumer engagement that can be a vital starting point for policy change. In fact, many US government policies are open for public comment before they are set into stone. US citizens can visit www.regulations.gov to find policies that are available for open comment. A similar process exists in many other countries, such as in the UK, where public comments are elicited through consultation, or green papers.

Sometimes, policy can even be directly related to fandom, as was the case with the Furthering Access and Networks for Sports (FANS) Act, proposed to the US Congress in 2015 but ultimately not passed. The bill would have increased access to broadcasted sports, regardless of one's physical location. Legislation is important not just for social issues at large, but also for how we as fans are allowed to legally engage in important fan-like acts, like fan art and fan fiction. Check out *Fandom and the Law: A Guide to Fan Fiction, Art, Film & Cosplay* by Marc H. Greenberg for a closer look at legislation impacting fan participation in fandom.

DONATING TIME OR MONEY (OR BOTH)

Create a list of charities and nonprofit organizations you have researched, and when you have a little extra money, send some their way. Many organizations have onetime or recurring donation options, and some are even working to accept donations in the form of Bitcoin and other cryptocurrencies. One of the perks of donating money is that it can be tax deductible, and employers will often match a portion of employee donations. It's worth checking with your employer to see if they will match a portion if you plan to make regular donations. And, as a recruitment and retention tool, more and more employers are building in days of service and paid leave time for employees to volunteer.

If you happen to work for your government, though, it might be important to investigate rules and regulations about fundraising and donations before committing to this type of action. For example, many federal employees in the United States can donate to partisan political campaigns but can't specifically fundraise for them or run for office. There may still, however, be matching campaigns for nonpartisan donations that you can take advantage of, such as the Combined Federal Campaign.

PBS (Public Broadcasting Service) and NPR (National Public Radio) are two US organizations funded by donations and also connected to fandom (*Doctor Who* first aired in the States on PBS, and NPR has helped fuel growth in the podcast industry). These media sources, along with the National Endowment for the Arts, are dependent on donations from the public rather than entirely funded by taxes and fees, as is the case with the BBC. We have included a list of sites to help you research donation matching options in the Resources section.

Use the space below to come up with a budget based on where you'd like to donate, how much you'd like to donate, and how much your employer will match:

Organization _____

Your Contribution _____

Employer Matching? ____ Yes   ____ No

Total Contribution _____

Organization _____

Your Contribution _____

Employer Matching? ____ Yes   ____ No

Total Contribution _____

Organization _____

Your Contribution _____

Employer Matching? ____ Yes   ____ No

Total Contribution _____

Organization _____

Your Contribution _____

Employer Matching? ____ Yes   ____ No

Total Contribution _____

Of course, if your budget is tight, you can also donate your time to a cause or organization you feel is important. Volunteer opportunities can be as simple as writing to a person who is being held in an immigrant detention center or staffing a booth at a local community event, and as involved as traveling abroad to serve with groups like Habitat for Humanity or Doctors Without Borders.[9] If in-person volunteering is challenging, there are many opportunities to volunteer online or from home. Check out the Resources list for more information.

---

9   While Doctors Without Borders is an amazing organization, there
      has been some discussion recently about whether service or mission
      trips—where people from wealthy industrialized countries go and build
      things or perform services abroad—are more harmful than good. A
      specific issue is whether wealthy volunteers take jobs away from local
      workers who need the income.

BOYCOTTING

The opposite of giving money or time is, well, not doing that. In an increasingly capitalist world where markets are extremely powerful, withholding your money or time from individuals, groups, corporations, or services that you disagree with is a powerful strategy.

You might be wondering why boycotting—refusing to spend money or use services in order to make a political point—is in a section on individual actions. Although boycotts are most effective if you can get a significant number of people to join, they start with you. And they can help you feel like you are in touch with and acting in accordance with your values. We'll discuss boycotting in more detail later, too.

BLOG, STREAM, SCREAM ABOUT IT

One of the best resources we have as individuals is our ability to communicate what we've learned with others. Get loud! You don't need to literally scream, but you can find ways to turn your individual voice into a resource for others. For example, the #FreeBritney movement started with a podcast, which gained a following that eventually drew enough public attention to help free pop star Britney Spears from a years-long conservatorship. The creators of the podcast didn't necessarily start out to create a movement; they were just discussing the singer-songwriter's Instagram account. But as they dove into the myth that is and surrounds Britney Spears, they learned more about the conservatorship, and conservatorships in general, while their podcast evolved. The movement has ultimately led to more eyes on the issues impacting those who experience mental illness and a larger examination of laws concerning conservatorships in California, where Spears's conservatorship was filed.

Sometimes just posting about something can earn us our own fan following. Take for example the work of Alexis Nikole Nelson, known on social media as the "Black Forager." Nelson did her research on an issue she cared deeply about: food foraging and the complex history it has in food traditions of BIPOC individuals. Nelson instructs viewers on how to identify and gather food sustainably in their own backyards, usually using humor and cute jingles. Nelson also teaches about the oppressions and liberations of BIPOC communities, bringing an important, often-overlooked perspective to environmental conservation. For instance, she encourages foraging large amounts of plants that are invasive and that threaten local indigenous ecosystems, and she teaches how to take only as much as needed or to replant species that might need a little extra help to thrive.

Digital civic engagement is particularly accessible to younger activists. This is perhaps because the tools are more familiar to younger users and can also be easily shaped by fan engagement. Digital civic engagement is the act of participating in the public sphere or politics via social media or other online activities. It can range from your local representative hosting a virtual town hall via Zoom, to K-pop fans flooding the White Lives Matter hashtag with videos of their favorite idols. TikTok, for example, gained leverage as a place for digital civic engagement after young users made it just that. The platform was originally about sharing self-expression and building community online through things like music and dance. When young people decided to express themselves through activism, however, it became something else entirely.

GET CREATIVE

As with blogging and streaming, art has a way of spreading. For example, most of us recognize anti-war art by Bansky, like *Rage, Flower Thrower*, or *Girl with Balloon*, even if we've never seen the original street paintings. Fan art can be just as prolific. Take for example Hayley Gilmore's protest art of Leia Organa with the words "A Woman's Place Is in the Resistance" superimposed over it. You've probably seen that art or something like it, given how widely it was shared and how often images of Leia were used in Women's Marches across the United States in 2017.[10] In addition to protest imagery, art can provide commentary on representation in media, which is its own form of activism in that it challenges the status quo and can help people who are otherwise marginalized feel seen.[11]

Creativity is the antithesis of oppression, so creation alone can be a radical act. Since art comes in many forms, there are multiple ways to create, including those specific to fandoms, like cosplay. Not all cosplay is activism, but cosplay that challenges norms in media or that holds a sociopolitical message can be. Activist cosplay is a lot like drag—socially subversive while also being a lot of fun.

SPEAK UP ABOUT MARGINALIZATION IN PHYSICAL SPACES

Speaking up in the face of marginalization is not easy. There are real risks. Speaking up can mean risking criticism, ostracization, gaslighting, bullying, and, in some cases, violence. Because of this, the prospect of speaking up might feel overwhelming. But speaking up becomes easier when you find your community because

10   For more on the use of Leia images in protest, see: Matthew Corkins, "Princess Leia Poster: Legal Issues Won't Keep This Artist Out of the Rebellion," *Observer*, February 17, 2017, https://observer.com/2017/02 /princess-leia-poster-legal-issues-wont-keep-this-artist-out-of-the -rebellion/.

11   For more on this, see: Tereza Walsbergerová, "Fanart Activism: Fan Participation as a Tool for Representation and Diversity Awareness," *Re:Views Magazine*, October 10, 2017, http://reviewsmagazine.net/fanart -activism-fan-participation-as-a-tool-for-representation-and-diversity -awareness/.

you'll have like-minded and/or similarly identified people standing with you if things go sour. This increases safety, but it also means that if you are shut down, you'll have others who can step up and repeat the message. For example, if convention staff shut down a question, someone else might step up to ask your question again.

If you are not someone who is marginalized in fandom spaces, consider where you might be able to ally with folks who are. Don't take away from their ability to stand up for their own representation, but if you see someone getting shut down, there may be an important opportunity to help that person by backing them up. If speaking up at conventions isn't your thing, there are lots of ways to speak up online. You can write for or contribute to blogs, participate in groups and forums, or share fan works that relate to the kinds of representation you are seeking. A huge component of the visibility of the Destiel ship (the romantic pairing name for Dean Winchester and the angel Castiel in *Supernatural*), for example, was the sharing of slash fan fiction[12] on platforms like Archive of Our Own (AO3). This included works by LGBTQIA+ fans that explicitly explored narratives about identity, such as stories of coming out or managing internalized homophobia or biphobia. In fact, at the time of writing this book, Destiel was the most visible ship on AO3, with over one hundred thousand works written about the pairing—a milestone celebrated by actor Misha Collins on Twitter, drawing even more attention to the ship. When you are speaking up, make sure you are doing so in a way that is non-harassing. It's okay to say you want better representation, but it's not okay to threaten or personally attack people. In fact, that can delegitimize the people who are advocating respectfully and can ultimately hurt a cause.

---

12   Slash fan fiction is fan fiction focused on the romantic or sexual pairing of two same-sex characters.

ATTEND A PROTEST

Sometimes your best resource as an activist is your physical body, so use it to attend peaceful protests related to a cause. You do not need to be involved in organizing a protest to attend, but you should engage in enough research ahead of time to know what the rules of engagement are. For example, where are protesters allowed to assemble? Will there be a police presence or the presence of counterprotesters? If you are concerned about being directly involved in a protest, look into opportunities to bring water, snacks, or sunscreen, or find other ways to support protesters. Large protests planned well in advance will sometimes have websites and social media pages with this information. For example, the 2017 March for Science, held in cities throughout the United States, had plentiful information available online about goals of the protests and where they would be held. At least one satellite location of the march, in San Jose, California, shared proximity with a fandom convention, Silicon Valley Comic-Con. The con was held at the San Jose McEnery Convention Center, just steps from where the march took place. As a result, fans, and at least one celebrity (Adam Savage, who was booked at the con), were able to attend both events simultaneously.

When attending a protest, it's important to prepare for the possibility of arrest and violence. This is not an inevitability, but it does happen. Luckily, there are ways to make sure any protest quests you engage in are as safe as they are revolutionary. For example, try to increase your situational awareness so you can exit before a tense situation gets worse, and scout out multiple routes to leave an area in case the most obvious routes become blocked. For those in the United States, check out the American Civil Liberties Union (ACLU)'s simple guide to knowing your rights to protest, found at www.aclu.org/know-your-rights/protesters-rights/. If you are not in the States, look into local legal organizations or online guides to learn more about your protest rights. And, as tear gas is a common hazard at protests, we also recommend checking out the guide that Physicians for Human Rights created, which you can find at phr.org/our-work/resources/preparing-for-protecting-against -and-treating-tear-gas-and-other-chemical-irritant-exposure-a -protesters-guide/.

The 2021 protest against the owners of Manchester United Football Club at the Old Trafford stadium caused the delay of a game and forced a dialogue about club ownership. If you aren't a sports fan and don't know what any of that means, don't worry! Basically, several of the top football clubs (that means soccer teams) in Europe sought to create a new super league. The move was criticized by fans for prioritizing profits over competition, and it resulted in protests by said fans.[13] One of the more successful of these was against the owners of Manchester United: protesters lined up outside a stadium and caused a game to be postponed, leading the owners to enter into a dialogue with fans about the proposed new league and overall ownership of the club.[14]

LOOK INTO FANDOM-SPECIFIC TASKS

Many fandoms have volunteer opportunities specific to the fandom itself. For example, many fan-based organizations need help with things like archiving information online, writing newsletters, getting the word out about various causes, and much, much

---

13   For more information, check out: Abhimanyu Sen, "Explained: What
      Is Europe's Controversial Super League?" *Quint World*, April 20, 2021,
      https://www.thequint.com/sports/football/what-is-the-newly-announced
      -european-super-league#read-more.

14   For more on this, check out: "Manchester United vs. Liverpool postponed
      after anti-Glazer fan protests at Old Trafford," *CNBC*, May 3, 2021, https://
      www.cnbc.com/2021/05/03/manchester-united-vs-liverpool-postponed
      -after-anti-glazer-fan-protests-at-old-trafford.html.

more. Look for tabs on fan websites that say things like "Jobs and Volunteering" or "Get Involved." If you don't see anything like that on a website, reach out to them through their "Contact Us" page. Fan organizations often have tables, booths, or other kinds of physical presence at in-person conventions where you can ask them about what opportunities there might be for you. If you aren't sure if you have time to volunteer for one of these fandom-based tasks, simply sharing information is an excellent way to get involved. The more a cause is shared, the more likely it is to get the attention needed to propel it forward. More eyes on something means more funds raised and more forces for good.

The best example of this can be found in true crime fandom. Many true crime fans have made good use of the accessibility of information via the internet to become amateur investigators themselves. They've used online resources to compile information about cold cases, which can then be turned over to the police or professional investigators to solve cases. Some podcasts, like Exactly Right Podcast Network's *The Murder Squad*, in which individual listeners are given cold case information and asked to put their curiosity to good use, have been created in partnership with investigators or former investigators. Many podcasts and related fandoms have also spotlighted organizations like End the Backlog, an organization with the mission of ensuring that the tragic backlog of rape kits across the United States can be processed. Sharing information about organizations may seem like a small task, but the kind of systemic change needed for organizations to be successful does not typically come without some measure of public outcry. Powerful people need to get involved—usually the ones we vote for—so the more people who see and subsequently care about an issue, the better. It is important, however, to be mindful about how information is shared. The amateur sleuthing of true crime fans has been criticized for sometimes getting in the way of investigations or for overfocusing on crimes committed against young white women while ignoring higher incidences of violence against BIPOC women. You won't always get everything right the first time, so be willing to hear constructive criticism as you progress in your activist work. And remember: criticism isn't a call to stop—it's a call to do even better.

SUPPORT YOUR LOCAL COMIC BOOK STORE

You are engaging in activism by simply supporting your local comic book store or other small businesses. This is an act of resistance in its own right because local businesses tend to directly and demonstrably contribute back to their communities, whereas corporations, even when they do give back, don't often have the same kind of community impact. Your patronage of small businesses may also contribute to larger activist efforts, as many locally owned comic book stores participate in charity and activism of their own. For example, when news broke that a school board in Tennessee unanimously voted to ban a Pulitzer Prize–winning graphic novel about the Holocaust, *Maus*, a locally owned comic book store in the San Francisco Bay Area, offered to send one hundred free copies of the novel to families in the county where the ban took place. After store owner Ryan Higgins's tweet about the offer went viral, the story was picked up by national and local news media outlets across the country. Comics Conspiracy sold out of *Maus*. Sales of *Maus* increased 753 percent in the last weeks of January 2022, and the book rose to number sixteen on Amazon's best sellers across all genres.[15]

15   For more information on the increase in sales, check out: Anna Kaplan, "Sales of 'Maus' Soar 753% in Last Week of January Following Ban by Tennessee School District," *Forbes*, February 4, 2022, https://www.forbes .com/sites/annakaplan/2022/02/04/sales-of-maus-soar-753-in-last-week -of-january-following-ban-by-tennessee-school-district/?sh=22ecab5a4cb7.

LOBBY THE POWERS THAT BE FOR BETTER REPRESENTATION IN FILM AND TELEVISION

Remember how important diverse characters like *Star Trek*'s Nyota Uhura are to social movements at large? Sometimes representation like that only happens through lobbying production studios, often labeled "The Powers That Be," or TPTB. So what gets the attention of TPTB? In short, the answer is numbers, reach, creativity, and persistence. In the age of the internet, this is easier than ever.

Wayward Daughters was initially created by fans Riley Santangelo and Betty Days as a social media campaign. Their aim was to create a women-centered spin-off of *Supernatural* with intersectional LGBTQIA+ and BIPOC representation. These efforts were strengthened by actor participation in championing the cause, resulting in greater awareness and even a backdoor pilot for a spin-off that, while not picked up for a series, did inevitably drive important parts of the show's plot in later seasons. By the final season of *Supernatural*, there were arguably more main queer characters than straight ones, as well as a whole host of women characters whose story arcs did not revolve only around being love interests. There was a Black woman character with a significant multi-season arc, and one of the main character's love interests was a deaf woman, played by a deaf actor. Another actor, diagnosed with multiple sclerosis, was given reasonable accommodations to make several appearances in the show's final seasons and also occupied a role significant to the overall plot.

EDUCATE OTHERS

Sometimes, just educating one person on a point of social justice can go a long way. This can be as simple as correcting someone who uses outdated language or sharing the little-known history of a group. It's important that you share new information in a way that is non-attacking and non-defensive. People don't learn new things very well if they feel threatened, which can be a difficult territory to tread as an activist passionate about a cause. Ask if someone is open to having a one-on-one conversation about the issue. It can help to start by sharing an example of when *you* messed up. This shows vulnerability and establishes that you don't expect the person you're speaking with—or anyone, for that matter—to be perfect. Keep it simple. Be clear that the goal of the conversation is learning, not judging. One idea is to start with a conversation about how a product you love may not have aged well or a situation where the product is still inspiring but the creator has become problematic (looking at you, Rowling and Whedon).

ENGAGE IN A RANDOM ACT OF KINDNESS

Have you ever been the recipient of an anonymous generous act? It is truly the best surprise! Actor Misha Collins credits a random act of kindness he and his family experienced when he was a child as the inspiration for his charitable work and activism. In several interviews, Collins has shared that, during a period of homelessness, his mother received a cash gift from a stranger that enabled her to purchase holiday gifts for Collins and his siblings.

There are several notable examples of the importance of a random act of kindness in geeky media as well. Consider young Peeta intentionally burning bread in order to throw it out so that a hungry Katniss could take it home to her family. This act of kindness shaped the rest of the story in *The Hunger Games*. Had Peeta not shown this kindness, Katniss may not have felt compelled to defy an authoritarian government to save him, ultimately sparking a political revolution that would change the entire country of Panem.

The most beautiful thing about fan activism and charity work is that, like random acts of kindness, the positive consequences of your actions—these "fandom acts of kindness"—can be widespread and can inspire others to do good. None of us gets through life without help from others. Even the most independent among us benefit from those who have gone before and worked, fought, struggled, and died for us to have better lives. As the world gets bigger, we have the challenge of and opportunity for global citizenship. What we do in our fan communities to help each other transcends into helping people we will never meet.

BE YOURSELF

Sometimes we help without even knowing it! By just being yourself, you make the world a better, more equitable place. For example, meeting other queer and nonbinary people within fandoms helped Kaela feel more comfortable exploring their own identities, something that Kaela now strives to pay forward by increasing their own visibility in both queer and fan spaces. Tanya loves bringing fandom and fan culture into the classroom. She's presented several panels on how to use fandom as pedagogy and is thrilled when attendees follow up with requests for the slides.

CHECK YOUR INVENTORY AND MOBILIZE

When gaming, you usually have an inventory of tools at your disposal, some that you start out with and others that you gain through experience. You can't win a big boss battle, or even complete a side quest, without some tools. Like checking your inventory in a game, in activism, you'll need to survey the tools at your disposal for collective action and use them to mobilize. For example, streaming platform Twitch and mobile game *Pokémon GO* have a built-in audience, are easy to use for quick dissemination of information, and, in the case of Twitch, have real-time streaming capabilities that can subvert efforts by governments or oppressive regimes to shut down protesters' means of communication with one another and the world at large. As such, they've served as important tactical tools for networking during many activist demonstrations, most notably the protests held in Hong Kong in 2019. It is impossible to believe a press release that says police brutality did not occur, after all, if the world witnessed that brutality live or via recordings on Twitch and other streams.

It's important to note that it's not just everyday fans who have learned the power of tools like Twitch to mobilize fandoms. Democratic US politicians Ilhan Omar and Alexandria Ocasio-Cortez, for example, used the Twitch platform, and the audience of internet personality Pokimane, to mobilize and engage with voters and their constituents while playing rounds of the popular game *Among Us*. In December of 2020, politician and voting rights activist Stacey Abrams similarly used social media tools to mobilize fans of *Supernatural* to raise money for the nonprofit Fair Fight. Abrams worked with several actors and show creator Eric Kripke to assemble fans for an online, convention-style panel and fundraiser. In addition to facilitating donations to Fair Fight, the event encouraged fans to exercise their right to vote.

Fundraising in particular is a tool commonly used in fan activism that benefits from knowing what's in your toolkit. Knowing what's available to you can help you to mobilize with like-minded fans around a common fundraising goal. This is true of online spaces like the ones discussed above, but also of in-person spaces like fan conventions. There is something really special about enjoying the thing you love with others who also love it. It's the reason we're willing to pay more and work harder to access an in-person event when we could just watch the movie, game, or concert for less money in the comfort of our own home. But experiencing that heightened emotion is like nothing else. Sociologist Émile Durkheim labeled this feeling "collective effervescence." We sometimes call it "shared feels." Gatherings and events, especially those linked to specific times of the year or rituals like weddings or baby showers, help us to affirm our values and build community. Fandom gatherings are no different. When we come together to celebrate our love of something, we enjoy the emotional intensity of collective effervescence. That feeling also motivates us and gives us the emotional energy to put into building community and trying to do good in the world—and can also inspire us to mobilize around charitable efforts.

From merchandise auctions to canned food drives, fandom gatherings bring in millions of dollars for charitable groups every year. If you have favorite fan events that you regularly attend, chances are there are already opportunities to donate directly to charity at the events. And, increasingly, fandom-based nonprofits have information booths or activities at conventions. If local events do not already have fundraisers, this may be an opportunity to partner with others and create them. Some comic book stores and other fandom-related organizations also have in-person and online fundraising options.

Once you have gained some experience points, leveled up, and checked your inventory, you can focus on finding, building, and/or leading a team. As was previously mentioned, teams are important for larger change. As Sora states in the RPG *Kingdom Hearts*, "Although my heart may be weak, it's not alone. It's grown with each new experience, and it's found a home with all the friends I've made. I've become a part of their heart just as they've become a part of mine. And if they think of me now and then . . . if they don't forget me . . . then our hearts will be one. I don't need a weapon. My friends are my power!" So let's discuss how to find your companions on this journey.

Chapter 4

JOINING A TEAM

"Everything we've done, we've done together. We got here together, and we're still here. Things have happened, but it's always worked out for us, 'cause it's always been all of us. That's how I know. 'Cause as long as it's all of us, we can do anything."
Rick Grimes, *The Walking Dead*, Season 6, episode 16

You've probably seen your fair share of pop culture zombies. From Russo and Romero (*Night of the Living Dead*) to Darabont and Kirkman (*The Walking Dead*), the key element of any good zombie story is the team the protagonist finds themselves fighting with. It's why the zombie genre endures. There are limitless stories to be told about using teamwork to rise above a common threat and, in the more hopeful narratives, to rebuild society better than it was before.

BEFORE YOU JOIN UP

When you are really passionate about a cause, it might seem like the skills, tools, or even solutions needed to effect change are obvious. It can be tempting to approach an existing organization like a zombie, with a "shoot first and ask questions later" kind of attitude, but that might be counterproductive and could actually undermine the efforts that others have been fine-tuning for years. Let's think about *The Walking Dead*'s Rick Grimes. When we first meet him, Rick has just woken up in a hospital, surrounded by chaos. He's been in a coma for two months and has missed the entire unfolding of the apocalypse around him. Rick is a cop and the presumed head of his family, so he's used to being in charge and used to charging in (it's literally how he ended up in the coma to begin with: stepping forward during a shoot-out while on duty as an officer). Rick does eventually become a leader, but he must first follow the organized groups he encounters because he doesn't know what they know about the zombies. Imagine if Rick hadn't listened to Morgan, who advised him to stay quiet while the house they were holed up in was surrounded by walkers. What would have happened if Rick hadn't listened to Glenn, who helped him escape the horde in Atlanta? Sure, it's Rick's plan that ultimately gets the group out of Atlanta, but he could only devise the plan because he deferred to the expertise of the people who had already been there, doing the work and evading the zombies.

Any group you join has a collective and institutional knowledge. You should approach new groups like you are waking up from a coma in the middle of the apocalypse because, metaphorically speaking, you probably are—especially if you're new to activism or to a given cause. It's likely that by the time you find a group, they'll already have been together for a while and will have already been gathering their own intel about a given issue.

That intel is important. It likely includes lessons learned about systemic barriers, plans that have been tried, and the success or failure rate of those plans. We encourage you to be mindful of that and to take the time to get to know what the group knows before positioning yourself in any place of authority on the matters at hand. We'll discuss leadership in the next chapter, but for now, remember that every good leader starts out as a follower. That's how you learn.

COLLECTIVE FUN

Okay, we all know this "group action" thing works for fighting zombies, but how and why does it work in the real world? More importantly, why join up with activist groups centered specifically around fandom as opposed to the tons of other groups out there doing similar work? In a word: it makes activism *fun*, and fun makes otherwise hard work sustainable. There is also something uniquely empowering about fandom as a collective. From a sociological perspective, the whys and hows of successful fan activism are because of the "Four Cs." The Four Cs of fandom-based activism and charity work are:

1. Collective Identity: Fans share an identity as members of a particular fandom
2. Collective Effervescence (aka Shared Feels): The excitement you feel when you're part of a crowd appreciating things together
3. Community: A social group distinguished by their enthusiasm for a particular fandom
4. Collective Action: Working together with others to accomplish a common goal

COLLECTIVE IDENTITY

In her dissertation on fan activism, Jamie Puglin (2020) posited that part of why fandoms are a great resource for collective action is because fans already share a collective identity. This shared identity is also already action-based through fan activities like creating and sharing fan fiction and fan art or attending conventions. In other words, being a fan isn't just something you *are*; it's something you *do*. To paraphrase one of our interviewees, it's the difference between being a fan with a lowercase "f" and being a Fan with an uppercase "F." This collective identity, then, can be called on to mobilize people to action.

COLLECTIVE EFFERVESCENCE

You know that feeling you get when you're at a live event, like when the entire movie theater loudly cheered as Cap summoned Mjölnir in *Avengers: Endgame*? That feeling is what sociologist Emile Durkheim calls "collective effervescence," and what we like to call "shared feels" (mostly because it's easier to spell). The collective emotional highs and lows we feel when we're sharing an experience, especially when we occupy the same physical space, eventually give rise to shared values and norms. One of the unique things about fandom is that, starting long before it was a regular part of society at large, fans have straddled virtual and physical community spaces. In fact, because so many fans were already connected to one another virtually through various social media platforms and were familiar with how tools like Twitch, Discord, and other gaming and streaming services could support opportunities for socialization, fan culture was particularly well positioned to foster social interactions online at the start of the COVID-19 pandemic.

Actor Alexander Siddig, best known for his role as Dr. Bashir on *Star Trek: Deep Space Nine*, hosted biweekly Zoom meetings for the "Sid City Social Club" during the spring of 2020. The meetings were capped at one hundred attendees and ran for about two hours each. Siddig would call on fans who wanted to chat and would spend anywhere from fifteen to thirty minutes casually talking. In this way, the Social Club meetings were just that—building community and helping fans feel connected by providing a way to experience collective effervescence outside of a physical convention. While there was a lot of general *Star Trek*–related conversation, there was also genuine conversation between Siddig and guests, which made the meetings feel more intimate than the typical celebrity/fan interactions you'd get at a convention.

COMMUNITY

The community that forms around a specific cause is the key to effective activism. Social movements began because people gathered in communities and worked to make change outside of the existing power structures. Church groups and student groups, especially those led by Black people in predominantly Black communities, were crucial for fostering and sustaining the Civil Rights Movement. Before the 1960s, not all citizens had the right to vote in the United States. And even when Black Americans were guaranteed the right to vote, they were often prevented from doing so, both overtly (racially oppressive poll taxes, literacy tests, all-white primary elections) and covertly (voter ID laws, difficult-to-access polling locations, limited voting machine availability in majority non-white districts). Because of this marginalization, people gathered where they were less oppressed and restricted. These locations then became centers of power. Fandom-based groups are similar in that many of their members have been marginalized or excluded from other communities. Women, BIPOC, LGBTQIA+ folks, disabled people, undocumented people, lower-income people, and other marginalized groups are often excluded from status quo political actions. Many interviewees we spoke with talked about finding familial-type relationships via fandom. Fandoms can become a chosen family for individuals estranged from their biological or legal families. Because of the way some pop culture products showcase same-sex individuals and couples, their fandoms attract large numbers of people who identify as part of the LGBTQIA+ community. Notable examples are Earpers (fans of *Wynonna Earp*) and Xenites (fans of *Xena: Warrior Princess*). At Xenite Retreat 2019, out of approximately 150 attendees, there were no fewer than five marriage proposals among same-sex couples! Many of the couples had met each other through the fandom. As one person put it, upon finding the *Supernatural* fandom: "I belong here."

It might not always be easy to find your community right away if you belong to a marginalized group. Potential friends and allies may not stand out immediately from the crowd, especially in convention spaces. In seeking out community, you might look for visual cues or language that suggests a moniker of safety. For example, in looking for fellow LGBTQIA+ fans at a convention, you might look for people with pins or shirts that reference a particular ship or for other hints of expression of LGBTQIA+ identities. In starting up a conversation, you might look out for language that suggests a safe space, or lack thereof—if shipping[16] is mentioned, even minimally, how do folks respond? Many larger convention spaces have booths and meetups specifically for people with marginalized identities to connect, and if you don't see what you're looking for at a particular convention, you can always create something yourself. For example, in the early years

---

16   Shipping: typically pairing two characters from a story in a romantic relationship

of *Supernatural* conventions, when it was taboo to discuss shipping, shippers created their own convention spaces. Don't have the bandwidth to create your own convention? You can also simply reach out to organizers at existing conventions and request that a meetup be added to the calendar of events. You can also use hashtags on social media to informally organize something that is not endorsed by the convention but that occurs in or around the convention space. Finding people online is a little easier, as you can use search terms to easily find existing groups or to build groups. Once you find one another, there are endless possibilities for pooling efforts in order to build bigger communities and increase visibility.

COLLECTIVE ACTION

Collective action is essentially exactly what it sounds like—people coming together and acting for a specific purpose. For fan activism, collective action is a means to an end. If you've ever signed a petition, joined in a boycott, or attended a march or protest, you've participated in collective action. The ends that activist groups advocate for are typically a social, cultural, or political change that benefits either a specific group or all of society. When thousands of students around the world walked out of class on September 20, 2019, to protest their governments' inaction with respect to addressing climate change, they engaged in collective action to call attention to what they considered a pressing issue. Not yet eligible to exercise their right to vote to send a message to elected officials, students used a classic activist tactic to make their voices heard. Sustained over time, collective action is what makes a social movement. Take for example the release of the "Snyder Cut" of DC's *Justice League*, which was released following sustained efforts by fans over several years. Among other things, that re-release of the film addressed a gaping Cyborg-shaped hole in the plot, giving fans a more nuanced and well-rounded portrayal of a Black character by making him crucial to the story instead of sidelining him. This in turn gave the actor who played Cyborg, Ray Fisher, a revitalized platform for his own activism related to Black representation in Hollywood.

Fandoms, with collective identity frames that define being a fan as implying action, and which engage with events that build community and provide emotional fuel by way of collective effervescence, are uniquely positioned to be effective at collective action. The Four Cs are precisely why fandom-based activist groups have been successful—not only at fundraising, but also at accomplishing specific types of social change.

TYPES OF ORGANIZATIONS AND EXAMPLES

It's important to think about what kind of group you want to be a part of and why. It makes sense to choose a group with which you already share a collective identity through fandom, but you also want to consider how much bandwidth you actually have for this work. Is this going to be a regularly occurring volunteer gig, or something you do only on occasion? Is this a group that is physically based near where you live or work, or something you'll participate in virtually? The list of possible decision points is endless, so think about what types of groups sound most appealing and what interests you about the work they have done. Use the space below to write down some organizations you would like to research or the types of organizations you are interested in working with:

_____

_____

_____

_____

_____

FANDOM-BASED NONPROFIT ORGANIZATIONS

Organized groups like Random Acts and Fandom Forward are not only the inspiration for this book—they're also the best examples of what differentiates modern fandom-based activism from its previous iterations. While fundraising and charitable donations have been a part of fan culture since the beginning, fandom-based nonprofit organizations (NPOs) represent a unique stage in the evolution of fan activism that parallels the establishment of social movements.

Random Acts

It all started with a tweet. In 2010, after a devastating earthquake struck Haiti, *Supernatural* actor Misha Collins called on his fan base to donate money to UNICEF's disaster relief program. Collins had cultivated a devoted following on the relatively new social media site Twitter with his playful, interactive persona. When fans raised over $30,000 in just a few days, Collins recognized the potential to channel fan passion toward social good. Inspired by having benefited from acts of kindness as a child, Collins founded the nonprofit organization Random Acts. Its first major project, the Jacmel Children's Center in Haiti, which serves as a home for orphaned children, was completed in 2013. Random Acts has since grown into a global presence and is run entirely by volunteers. Collins still serves as president of the board of directors, but

Rachel Miner, a costar of Collins's on *Supernatural*, took over as executive director in 2018. In 2015, Random Acts built a free high school in Nicaragua for rural families, especially women, who may have a difficult time completing school after having children. The organization continues to fund the free school, sponsors food equality initiatives around the world, awards grants to classrooms and local initiatives, helps to staff and support a mental health crisis hotline, and partners yearly with Collins's scavenger hunt, GISH.

One of the explicit purposes of Random Acts is to inspire others to engage in service work and acts of kindness, but just like when a person throws a stone into a pond, or when a couple of hunters save someone's life, it can be difficult to observe all the places that kinetic energy touches. In *Supernatural*, for example, Dean frees Crowley in Season 9. Later, Crowley sacrifices himself to complete a critical spell in Season 12. This leads to the safe birth of the Nephilim (Jack) who will eventually restore the balance of the universe in Season 15. In other words, ripple effects can literally right the universe! Research supports the idea that engaging in service work leads to more acts of service and that, overall, volunteering is associated with significant, measurable increases in overall happiness. That said, there are likely many amazing acts of service inspired by others' work that are not being tracked.

Fandom Forward (Formerly Known as the Harry Potter Alliance)

Fandom Forward is a great example of how collective identity can be constructed in a way that precipitates activism. Andrew Slack, Seth Reibstein, and Sarah Newberry cofounded the Harry Potter Alliance in 2005 with members of wizard rock band Harry and the Potters. Slack and the band had performed together, often collecting donations for Amnesty International. What began as a way to raise awareness about social justice issues and get young people involved in activism using the framework of Harry Potter eventually morphed into a multi-fandom organization with chapters in thirty countries around the world. One of Fandom Forward's earliest campaigns, Dumbledore's Army, worked to stop the genocide in Darfur, asking fans to consider: What would Dumbledore do? Fandom Forward relied on the power of characters like Dumbledore, Harry, Hermione, and Neville to frame and motivate fan activism. The characters were used as celebrity motivators in this sense—we return to this point when we discuss celebrity involvement. Later campaigns ranged from lobbying Warner Bros., the studio behind the *Harry Potter* film franchise and merchandising, to use fair trade chocolate in the manufacturing of *Harry Potter*–themed candy, to the creation of Accio Books, an annual book drive that has collected and donated over five hundred thousand books to date.

FOR-PROFIT GROUPS: GISH

You might remember GISH from chapter one. Beyond the charitable work and good trouble that Gishers get into, it's just plain *fun*. It encourages creativity, kindness, and stepping out of one's comfort zone. Because the weirdness and social norm breaking is all in the name of the greater good, however, it enables participants to do things they wouldn't otherwise. Engaging in this kind of positive deviance helps to make seemingly impossible tasks fun and gives participants a sense of agency. Having fun and feeling like what you are doing makes a difference is crucial for sustaining any kind of activism or service work. The social issues and injustices that Gishers and other fan activists take on can feel overwhelming and disempowering. By gamifying social good, GISH, like Fandom Forward, has tapped into one of the key resources of fandom-based activism: activism is not easy, but it can be fun.

Gishers have raised hundreds of thousands of dollars through the power of social networking for the annual hunt's "Change a Life" item. This item typically consists of collecting donations to, quite literally, change lives. In 2018, $250,000 raised by fans participating in GISH was used to fund housing, food, and medical care for four Syrian refugee families, as well as schooling for the children of those families. Other "Change a Life" items have ranged from funding a dance school in South Africa to supporting an Afghani children's hospital. Although GISH is technically a for-profit corporation, most of the money raised goes to support charitable initiatives.

FUNDRAISING GROUPS

The line between fundraising and activism can be blurry. For example, each year, fans around the world make and upload videos asking other fans to make donations to specific charities. Started by John and Hank Green in 2007, Project for Awesome (P4A) is a forty-eight-hour telethon-style livestream that raises money for a variety of charities. Originally intended to hack prioritization algorithms and get fan videos on YouTube's front page, P4A has collected millions for charity over the years. In 2019, the Young Democrats of America officially honored P4A. P4A's parent organization, the Foundation to Decrease World Suck, is more of a fundraising organization than an activist organization. Like other fandom-based nonprofits and organizations, it does amazing and impressive work, but it seems to be less focused on training people to do activism than other organizations are. Its goals of raising money may very well be activist in nature, but the fans themselves are more supportive of, rather than determining and taking action to bring about, said goals. That said, fundraising and donation campaigns are possibly one of the oldest types of fan activism. From the early days of conventions, fans have collected canned goods and money for various causes.

An example of a fandom-based fundraising group is the AUSXIP's Greater Good subsite. AUSXIP, or Australian Xena Information Page, is a fan-run website dedicated to Australian fans of the TV series *Xena: Warrior Princess*. Since the show's beginning, fans have raised money to support those in need; these actions are often referred to as being in service of "the greater good," a reference to a Season 1 episode in which Gabrielle has to impersonate Xena to save a village. AUSXIP sponsors auctions of merchandise and memorabilia each year and has raised millions for the favored charities of lead actors Lucy Lawless (Xena) and Renee O'Connor (Gabrielle): the Starship Foundation, which supports children's health care in New Zealand, and the House of Bards, a nonprofit theater company in San Pedro, California. Several other fandom-based fundraising groups follow similar strategies. Another notable example is the historic fundraising by fans of K-pop group BTS in 2020. After the band pledged to donate one million dollars to organizations affiliated with Black Lives Matter, fans—who refer to themselves as BTS's "ARMY"—matched the group's donation in less than twenty-eight hours!

GRASSROOTS ACTIVISM

"Grassroots" simply means starting from the source. Grassroots *activism* is an organization or movement that starts small and grows through collective action based on community needs, driven by community leadership and interests. Much of what's discussed in this chapter started out as grassroots efforts that later grew into something bigger. But grassroots group efforts might also involve brief, collective action started by an individual or a small group familiar with activist tactics at large. For example, the BTS ARMY disrupted the identification of Black Lives Matter protesters on a police website by flooding the reporting application with fancams, videos highlighting a single K-pop idol while performing live. That effort was started by one fan's tweet and was quickly shared, and acted on, by a huge number of fans.[17] The best way to make sure you see grassroots efforts in real time is to follow top fan accounts on social media and the fans that other fans are following. These are the accounts most likely to initiate or spread grassroots efforts.

CELEBRITY INVOLVEMENT

Celebrities will often leverage their popularity to draw attention to causes, participate in activism, or encourage charitable work or volunteerism. We call these high-profile figures Starticipants, a portmanteau of "star" and "participant." Starticipants are unique in that they intentionally interact with fans in a way that both produces the emotional energy needed for activism and helps to focus fandom communities on specific goals.

For years, celebrities have used their individual platforms to advocate for charitable causes. In more recent years, with the onset of social media, sites like Omaze incentivize giving donations by offering prizes like set visits and lunches with your favorite stars. However, Starticipants are distinct from stars who participate in these kinds of raffles, as well as from stars who act as spokespeople, in significant ways. Firstly, Starticipants intentionally construct their public persona in dialogue with their fans. Secondly, Starticipants are part of the collective identity process that defines both the Starticipant leader and the participant fan.

---

17   For more information on this protest tactic, check out: Zoe Haylock, "K-Pop Stans Spammed the Dallas Police Department's App with Fan Cams," *Vulture*, June 1, 2020, https://www.vulture.com/2020/06/k-pop -stans-crashed-dallas-police-app-with-fan-cams.html.

Starticipants work to create their own fandom-based nonprofit organizations, while other celebrities often work with existing organizations. That's a good thing, of course! However, we think the creation of fandom-based organizations is a significant sign that fan activism is becoming a social movement. Finally, Starticipants not only help to focus a critical mass of active fans toward charity work; they also have the potential to bring in other Starticipants.

Arrow star Stephen Amell, for example, launched successful charity T-shirt campaigns in 2014 to raise awareness and money for cancer prevention and treatment, an anti-bullying organization (Stand for the Silent), and animal-assisted therapy for veterans (Paws and Stripes). Amell was later joined by fellow CW actor and *Supernatural* star Jared Padalecki, who started the Always Keep Fighting campaign to raise money and funds to address mental illness and the stigma surrounding it. In 2016, *Supernatural* stars Misha Collins and Jensen Ackles ran their own T-shirt campaign to fund training for volunteers at an online crisis hotline. The hotline is facilitated by suicide prevention group IMAlive but is supported by partnerships through Random Acts and is in part staffed by volunteers recruited and trained through the *Supernatural* fandom.

It may be difficult to contact and partner with a Starticipant. While Starticipants are important for moving fan activism beyond the boundaries of fandom, Starticipant participation is just a contributing factor, not a sufficient cause, for fandom-based action. Prominent fans within the community or even fictional characters can also play the role of Starticipant. As mentioned, Fandom Forward was built in part by reconstructing Harry, Hermione, Neville, Dumbledore, and other characters as Starticipants. A quick internet search of your fandom's or Starticipant's name and "charity work" may lead you to existing fan activist organizations.

You could also ask prominent fans or post in social media spaces for help with connecting to charitable organizations. People in fan activist spaces want to be helpful. If you interact politely, and in good faith, most folks will point you in the right direction.

So now that you have knowledge and, hopefully, experience in fandom-based nonprofits, it's time you took on a leadership role in activism.

Chapter 5

LEADERSHIP

"Water. Earth. Fire. Air. Long ago, the four nations lived together in harmony. Then everything changed when the Fire Nation attacked. Only the Avatar, master of all four elements, could stop them. But when the world needed him most, he vanished. A hundred years passed, and my brother and I discovered the new Avatar, an airbender named Aang. And although his airbending skills are great, he has a lot to learn before he's ready to save anyone. But I believe Aang can save the world."

Katara, *Avatar: The Last Airbender*, opening sequence

As the Avatar, Aang is expected to master bending the four elements of water, earth, fire, and air while others can bend only one. While Aang does eventually become proficient in bending all of these elements, it could be argued that his real power is in uniting the people of the world—including members of the Fire Nation—to end the tyranny of Fire Lord Ozai. And even more impressively, he does so not by killing Ozai but by disempowering him. It isn't Aang alone who brings balance, however; it is through the efforts of Team Avatar and the coalition of people from all nations working together that positive change is achieved. This is effective leadership: leading through teamwork, not through power.

LEADING BY EXAMPLE

The goal of activism is, through collective action, to dismantle systems and institutions that are diametrically opposed to your cause. To do so, leadership needs to be as decentralized as possible so that the oppressed do not become the oppressors if and when a movement gains momentum. This is what we love about the way Aang leads. Aang acts as a rallying force, not as the sole arbiter of the final conflict. Team Avatar participates in something that activist scholars refer to as "prefigurative organizing," which simply refers to leading or governing within an organization using the type of power structure you are ultimately working toward. The Avatar team worked toward a more egalitarian way of life, which meant their tactics also needed to be egalitarian and could not mirror Ozai's hierarchical approach.

Decentralized power in activist leadership can be as simple as having rotating facilitators for meetings, setting term limits for leaders, or having clear ways for group members to share feedback and ideas. There may still be times, such as when a time-limited decision needs to be made, for a leader to act alone. But those decisions are made in the best interests of the group, not in the best interests of the leader. In a nonhierarchical model, leadership is seen as a role rather than as an individual identity held by only one or a select few. Leading in this way also means sharing the tools of leadership instead of hoarding power. If a group would fall apart without its leader, it's not very effective. Everyone should have the same tools as the leader so that anyone could assume a leadership role, and those in leadership roles should strive to uplift those who are the most marginalized in their communities.

BECOMING A LEADER

There are many ways to find yourself in a leadership role. You might be elected or hired into a formal role by applying at an existing organization. You might become the de facto leader, or you could find yourself in a temporary leadership role if someone else vacates it and you happen to have the necessary knowledge to do the tasks needed. You may also find yourself in a leadership role by starting something new.

STARTING A LOCAL CHAPTER OF AN ORGANIZATION

Aside from the fact that a fairly well-known, existing organization can give you immediate access to recognizable branding for recruitment and establishing legitimacy, there are several practical advantages to joining or starting a local chapter of an established fandom-based nonprofit. First, there's far less paperwork and navigating the maze of bureaucracy than there would be if you were starting your own nonprofit. When starting your own nonprofit from scratch, you need to register it or otherwise ensure that you are complying with all state and federal guidelines. So, because existing organizations have already been through that process, they will already have systems in place to take care of the bulk of those responsibilities. Second, in starting a local offshoot you are tapping into an existing activist network. And because it comes with access to a group of passionate, like-minded fans, it probably also comes with some groundwork laid out for you to network with other charitable organizations. Finally, joining an established group can help sustain the organization over time. One of the challenges with nonprofit work and activism is volunteer burnout and turnover. Something like 30 percent of nonprofits fail within ten years.[18] Existing nonprofit organizations that have been around for a while will likely have found ways to overcome the high rate of failure. If nothing else, having access to a distributed network of a large number of volunteers means you won't have to do most of the work yourself. Check out the Resources section to find chapter information for each of these organizations and for information on other fandom-based nonprofit groups.

STARTING YOUR OWN NONPROFIT

One does not simply walk into Mordor, and one does not simply start a nonprofit organization. Sure, you can do it, but it is a lot of work—and you're going to want a solid fellowship of nerds to back you up.

The biggest advantage of starting a nonprofit is that you will be in control of the exact name and mission of your organization. You'll have the opportunity to build exactly the kind of organization you're looking for. That said, starting this campaign is like

---

18   Data on nonprofit closure and failure is complex. Some nonprofits may close because they transition into a different organization or because they accomplished their mission. Rates of "failure" are based on evaluating IRS tax-exempt filing status; this misses many small nonprofits that do not make enough money to apply for this status. For more on this, see: The NCCS Project Team, "The Nonprofit Sector in Brief," National Center for Charitable Statistics, June 4, 2020, https://nccs.urban.org/publication/ nonprofit-sector-brief-2019#finances; and Tracy S. Ebarb, "Nonprofits Fail—Here's Seven Reasons Why," National Association of Nonprofit Organizations & Executives, September 7, 2019, https://nanoe.org/ nonprofits-fail/#:~:text=The%20real%20data%20from%20National,of%20 a%20strategic%20plan%2C%20among.

being a first-time DM; it's a lot more work than it looks. Before you apply for tax-exempt status, you'll need to decide on your organization's name, your board of directors, and your bylaws. Use the space below to brainstorm some ideas for your organization's name, board, and potential bylaws. For an example of formal bylaws and other tips on starting a nonprofit, visit https://nonprofitally.com/start-a-nonprofit/nonprofit-bylaws/.

Potential Organization Names: _____

_____

_____

Potential Members of the Board of Directors: _____

_____

_____

Potential Bylaws: _____

_____

_____

The specific details around creating a nonprofit vary from state to state and country to country, and most experts recommend finding a lawyer or legal services professional that can help you navigate the particulars of your location. Typically, in the United States, the first step is filing the name of your organization with your state, and then later filing your articles of incorporation. Nolo.com has a resource hub with information on filing in all fifty states. For more on Nolo, see the Resources page at the end of the book.

COALITION BUILDING

As Team Avatar showed us, coalitions are powerful. Effective activism is often achieved through coalition building. By coalition, we mean an alliance of interested groups, individuals, political parties, and stakeholders who work together to accomplish a common goal. When multiple labor unions join to endorse or protest specific legislation or candidates, they are representing a coalition. While coalitions are often temporary, in the case of advocacy or activism, they can form longer-lasting commitments.

For example, Nerdfighters, P4A, and the charitable groups that receive the collected funds form a mutually beneficial coalition. Fandom Forward is excellent at partnering with and brokering alliances between different fandom and non-fandom-based groups to accomplish mutual goals. Many nonprofits will have a section on their website detailing groups and organizations that they frequently collaborate with.

If you are at a loss for where to start with coalition building, you might try brainstorming stakeholders. Who is actively involved? What might be some effective ways to partner with them or engage them in your campaign? Are there existing organizations in your community that might be interested in partnering with you? Reaching out to folks already active in your fandom community for suggestions may also help. Use the space below to identify potential stakeholders and ways to engage them.

Who are the main stakeholders for your cause?

_____

_____

_____

How can you partner with them?

_____

_____

_____

Community organizations to reach out to:

_____

_____

_____

STAKEHOLDER ANALYSIS

Once you have identified stakeholders, it's important to strategize how you will ask for change. Even the best ideas usually face some opposition, and understanding the needs and wants of stakeholders is one way to prepare for and tackle opposition when it arises, as well as to draw on the strengths of your allies. A critical tool used by a lot of project managers in change-based projects is a grid called a power/interest matrix.[19] The grid helps you identify how to engage stakeholders based on their level of power and interest in the change you are proposing.

---

19   For more information on the power/interest matrix and how it's
     used, see: Marie Slabá, "Stakeholder Power-Interest Matrix and
     Stakeholder-Responsibility Matrix in Corporate Social Responsibility,"
     The 8th International Days of Statistics and Economics, September 2014,
     1366–74, https://msed.vse.cz/msed_2014/article/358-Slaba-Marie-paper.pdf.

As helpful as this tool is, there is another way to approach stakeholder analysis that you might find a bit more fun: thinking of your stakeholders as players in a game of *Dungeons & Dragons*. In this method, the traditional stakeholder analysis is like your twenty-sided die; it determines what actions you can take and who holds the most power in a given setting or situation. The character alignments will give you an idea of how to personalize your strategy when engaging with those who hold power. In this case, we are using the "good," "neutral," and "evil" alignments to signify those for your cause (good), undecided about your cause (neutral), or against your cause (evil). (Not that anyone you are working with is literally evil.) Evil in this case just means "against your cause"—a sort of adversary who may have very good, rules-based, or personal reasons to oppose you, but who opposes you nonetheless. Try to work with these perceived adversaries whenever possible, recognizing that you yourself may occupy the same alignment for someone else's cause. Since we're talking about systemic change and not necessarily about battling the superpowered or supernatural, we've included some character examples from *Parks and Recreation*.

Following Aang's example, it's important to be an effective leader by modeling the change you want to see in the world and deferring to others' expertise when appropriate. One of the interesting things about the lore of some of our favorite fandom stories—from *Avatar* to *Avengers* to *Star Trek*—is the shared and rotating leadership of teams. James Holden from *The Expanse* becomes a more effective leader over the course of the series by learning to share responsibility with and seek input from the crew. After being thrust into an unwanted leadership position, Holden reacts emotionally, seeking vengeance. He learns to temper those impulses by trusting his crew, especially Naomi, and along the way institutes a participatory democracy of sorts on the *Rocinante*. Holden still serves as the ship's captain, but decisions

STAKEHOLDERS AS CHARACTER ALIGNMENTS

Lawful Good

Likely to see the good in your plan so long as it follows the rules. You want to appeal to the ways in which your plan advances the greater good while still abiding by or improving existing rules and regulations.

Character Examples:
Leslie Knope

Neutral Good

Likely to see the good in your plan simply because it is for the greater good. You want to appeal to the ways in which your plan advances the greater good. Rules and regulations may be relevant, but they are less important than the general appeal to goodness.

Character Examples:
Ann Perkins

Chaotic Good

Likely to see the good in your plan and willing to break rules if need be (rebels for the cause). You want to appeal to the ways in which existing rules that stand in your way run counter to your cause and, therefore, the greater good. You want to appeal to the reasons some rules should be broken.

Character Examples:
Andy Dwyer

Lawful Neutral

Undecided and governed by rules and organization. Think bureaucrats. You want to appeal to the ways in which your plan abides by or is based on existing rules and regulations. You need not appeal to why your cause is good—just to how it does not disrupt the existing order.

Character Examples:
Chris Traeger

True Neutral

Undecided wild cards that can be swayed for or against your cause. You want to appeal to the reasons why your plan will not require them to do a lot of work, or why it will benefit them in some way.

Character Examples:
April Ludgate

Chaotic Neutral

Undecided free spirit. You want to appeal to the reasons why your plan will help them maintain their own freedom.

Character Examples:
Tom Haverford

Lawful Evil	Neutral Evil	Chaotic Evil
Against your cause because it upsets existing rules/order. You want to find common ground within the rules: Where do your values overlap within the bounds of the rules?	Against your cause because it doesn't serve them. You want to find a way that your cause can serve them personally.	Against your cause, passionately. These are people who fundamentally oppose your cause and are unlikely to be swayed. You can try to appeal to ways in which your cause can serve them personally, but you may need to go above them, if that is an option.
Character Examples: Tammy 1	**Character Examples:** Jeremy Jamm	**Character Examples:** Tammy 2

are made by consensus with input from everyone. With a crew comprised of Earthers, Martians, and Belters, Holden's leadership represents the potential for humanity to work together despite a history of conflict between the groups. Having learned that the goal is more important than the means, Holden makes a surprising decision at the end of the TV series. When he is put in charge of the newly formed interplanetary alliance to regulate transportation to new worlds, he immediately resigns and gives the leadership position to Camina Drummer, a Belter, because he knows the importance of empowering the historically marginalized community in this context. Holden's willingness to abdicate leadership in order to accomplish a greater goal is exactly what makes him effective as a coalition builder throughout the series.

Chapter 6

LIVING IN A MATERIAL WORLD

"I don't want to sell anything bought or processed; or buy anything sold or processed; or process anything sold, bought, or processed; or repair anything sold, bought, or processed. You know, as a career, I don't want to do that."
Lloyd Dobler, *Say Anything*

Fandom is consumption. To fan over something is to consume a product. That product can be practically anything: music downloads, live sporting events, television streaming services, opening night tickets to see a new film featuring your favorite actor or franchise. This book is a product. And as a fan, you have consumed quite a few products, both fan-made and mass produced, that are related to the things that you love.

So what does consumption have to do with fan activism? The simple answer is that money holds power, and we all know that "with great power comes great responsibility." A lot of activism, particularly fan activism, is based on raising money for organizations or causes. While this is often done through direct donations, many charities and movements take advantage of consumer culture by selling things. Activism can also be a response to consumerism; you can choose to consume in a way that is more sustainable and in line with your values. In the case of fan activism, this can also mean the establishment or reinforcement of group norms about consumption that further a particular cause. Let's explore how you can be more ethical in your consumption of fandom media and goods.

WHAT IS ETHICAL CONSUMPTION?

Ethical consumption (sometimes called "ethical consumerism") can mean many different things. Are you concerned about the impacts of your consumption on global climate change? What about the materials that went into making a product—are they organic or sustainably made? And the people who made that product—were they paid appropriately for their labor and treated fairly? Finally, what about getting that product to you—was your product shipped from outside of your local community? How do we consider the cost of shipping in terms of both labor and carbon imprint? These are all valid and important questions when it comes to consumption of fandom products, goods, and services. Below are some thoughts for considering your fandom consumption and some tips to help you make choices more aligned with your values.

Ethical consumption is being intentional and deliberate in your consumption of goods and services in order to advocate for products and production practices more in line with social justice goals. Most of us live in advanced capitalist markets. Typically, we are quite removed from the process of production, as well as from the business practices of those responsible for the delivery of goods and services. Because our politics and policies (at least in the United States) are so influenced by what is assumed to be good for economic growth, sometimes one of the most powerful identities we have is that of the consumer. Corporations have figured out that fans and fan culture are huge markets to exploit. As fan activists, it's important to practice ethical consumption whenever possible. This can include some or all of the strategies outlined in this chapter. That's right: if you consider how using your power can be a way to advocate for social justice, even shopping can be an act of fan activism.

HOW TO RESEARCH CORPORATIONS

First, you need to identify what you are looking for: i.e., what business practices are most important to you in your own consumption of goods and services. As saturated as the global market is, it's nearly impossible to always hold all corporations responsible for every detail about production, sales, or service delivery that is important to you. A corporation might, for example, have excellent practices when it comes to supporting LGBTQIA+ employees, but have questionable practices when it comes to the use of sustainable materials or energy efficiency. You are also, presumably, human, and you are probably going to cave at some point and buy something from a business with practices you aren't thrilled with—either because you simply want something and have the means to get it, or because you don't have any other options to meet your needs. We all do it, even if we don't openly talk about it.

When looking for what kinds of business practices corporations engage in, the internet is your friend! One of the first places to start is the corporation's website. Corporations that are serious about social and environmental responsibility will typically share that on their website. Of course, this is not an unbiased source. Many corporations engage in something called "virtue signaling," a practice in which a company claims to support a particular cause while actually engaging in business practices that are the antithesis of that cause. For example, a corporation may claim to support LGBTQIA+ rights during Pride Month in June but donate money to anti-LGBTQIA+ organizations and politicians throughout the rest of the year. This specific kind of virtue signaling, in which companies slap a rainbow on something to make money while not actually caring about causes that are important to LGBTQIA+ people, is sometimes called "rainbow capitalism."

Rainbow capitalism is on full display in Season 2 of Eric Kripke's television series *The Boys*, based on Garth Ennis and Darick Robertson's wickedly satirical comic series of the same name. In the series, superheroes are manufactured and commercialized by a corporate entity named Vought. When one of Vought's most popular heroes, a woman who uses the moniker Queen Maeve, is outed as bisexual by a colleague (Homelander), Vought seeks to use her relationship with her girlfriend to sell products—with no concern for Maeve's actual relationship or actual identity. The company rebrands her as "Brave Maeve" and slaps her image with rainbow flags on a number of products. But because it worries that the market won't respond positively to Maeve's bisexuality, Vought engages in the harmful practice of bisexual erasure and refers to her as a lesbian. Vought, like other real-life companies, aims to profit from Maeve and her partner's relationship without doing the work to actually understand or truly further the representation of LGBTQIA+ people in a meaningful, productive way. Vought's website would likely be all rainbows, but the company probably wouldn't hold up to any real scrutiny about their values as a company.

As virtue signaling is a common practice, the mission is to determine if corporations are actually doing the things they say they are. Third-party verification or endorsement can be helpful. Several industries have nonprofit organizations that regulate and/or certify ethical production. A great example is fair trade certification. In order to qualify for fair trade status, businesses must undergo certification by an independent organization. Fair trade certification helps small farmers negotiate for fairer wages and labor practices, considers environmental impacts, and helps prevent child labor. Over 35,000 products are fair trade certified.

Use the space below to write down some of your favorite brands or media franchises, and compare what their websites say about their racial or social justice practices, labor practices, LGBTQIA+ support, or environmental ethics against what their scores are on third-party websites. We have compiled a list of sites to help you research companies. You can find that list in the Resources section.

Brand/Company/ Franchise	What Their Website Says:	Third-Party Score/ Evaluation:

SUPPORTING SMALL BUSINESSES AND INDEPENDENT ARTISTS

In 2010, American Express created Small Business Saturday as an alternative to Black Friday and Cyber Monday. The day supports smaller businesses and encourages local shopping, which keeps money in a community. Small Business Saturday was an instant hit and has since been held annually on the Saturday after Thanksgiving. Many communities have jumped on the Small Business Saturday bandwagon and extended the event into a week or several weekends leading up to the holidays. Chances are, if you live in a community with a downtown area, retailers near you participate in Small Business Saturday. Your local chamber of commerce branch likely sponsors this event and is a good resource to help you find small local businesses in general. You can also find small businesses through your neighborhood newsletters and social media pages.

Use the space below to write down some small local businesses near you:

_____

_____

_____

_____

_____

One of the best ways to support small businesses is by shopping on Etsy. That said, in recent years corporate vendors have also set up Etsy shops. Generally, if you read up on the company you are considering shopping with, however, you can determine the type of business it is. Many Etsy creators will also have an

Instagram account, where you can find more information and get in touch. One advantage of Etsy is that more of the money you spend will go to the creators—and, of course, you can find some truly amazing items. If an artist or Etsy creator does not have quite what you're looking for, you can also message them and ask if they would consider a custom design. Talking directly to the creator also provides a chance to ask about their sustainability initiatives and the details of their material sources. While Etsy remains one of the most popular marketplaces for small business, it does charge a commission, so you could also look for other platforms to find fan artists. Another popular site for fan art is Redbubble, which sells art prints: on shirts, bedding, coffee mugs, stickers, and more. Many artists will also share preferred methods for consumption on their social media feeds or individual websites.

Use the space below to write down some creators you can patronize and signal-boost to other fans:

_____

_____

_____

_____

_____

Most conventions will have a show floor or vendor area. Check out the booths selling unique handmade or -crafted items. Sometimes these are located in what's called or labeled "Artist Alley." Many artists and shops there will have social media information so that you can follow their releases and upcoming plans. Often, you can find artists actively drawing, painting, or crafting at their booths. It's pretty amazing to see the process and get to meet the person whose work you admire.

BLACK-OWNED BUSINESSES

When thinking about ethical consumption, it's also important to consider who owns the business you're patronizing. In addition to advocating for criminal justice reform, the Black Lives Matter movement also called on consumers to actively support Black-owned businesses, especially those struggling financially during the pandemic. One place to get started in finding Black-owned businesses is the Official Black Wall Street app, available in the Apple's App Store (more info at obws.com). There, you can find local businesses and restaurants, as well as online businesses, and you can read and leave reviews. Quick Google searches can also help you find Black-owned businesses in your area and online. Etsy and other platforms also feature lists of Black-owned shops.

Use the space below to identify Black-owned businesses in your area that you can patronize and signal-boost to others:

_____

_____

_____

_____

_____

BOOKSTORES

There's nothing quite like the smell of a bookstore—the scents of paper, ink, coffee, and freshly baked goods enfolding you in their warmth as you come in from the chill of a crisp fall day.

Tanya wrote most of her master's thesis sitting in a Borders bookstore (RIP Borders!). We're not psychic, but we're going to use our ESP/Betazoid senses and guess that you like reading and buying books. As avid nerds and bibliophiles, it would be remiss of us not to include a section on bookstores!

Though Amazon was founded as an online textbook and academic book store, it has quickly become a life-changing shopping experience. But it has also irrevocably changed the consumer goods and manufacturing industries and been the subject of serious labor practice complaints, especially in its distribution centers, where attempts at unionization have largely been unsuccessful. Like many massive, multinational corporations, Amazon has also contributed to the closure of small and local businesses and has an enormous carbon footprint. Why include Amazon in this list? Because, for many of us, it may be our only viable option for acquiring needed goods. The site's Amazon Smile portal enables you to select a charity and donate a portion of what you spend on Amazon.com to that group. The 0.5 percent of your purchases may seem small, but it can add up quickly and make a difference. Over one million charities participate in Amazon Smile, from well-established groups to smaller, local groups like churches and elementary schools. Fandom-based nonprofits Random Acts and the Critical Role Foundation are two geeky charities you can designate as beneficiaries.

Use the space below to identify charities or nonprofit organizations to search for on Amazon Smile:

_____

_____

_____

Bookshop.org is an excellent alternative to Amazon. It's an online bookstore that combines the convenience of Amazon with the ability to support small, independent bookstores. Shoppers can designate a bookstore to receive the profits of their purchases. Using this site, you can support local bookstores or Black-owned bookstores even if you don't live in an area with those resources. You can purchase books in various formats, including e-book, paperback, and hardcover. Prices are slightly higher than Amazon and shipping takes a bit longer, but overall, it's a great resource, and Bookshop has raised over $17 million for local bookstores.

It's hard to beat your local brick-and-mortar bookstore. If you live in a large enough metro area, chances are there's a great resource waiting to be discovered. Some of these brick-and-mortars directly support marginalized communities. For example, many LGBTQIA+ neighborhoods in large cities have bookstores that sell books written by and for the LGBTQIA+ community. Some bookstores have direct ties to activist work, such as San Francisco's Bound Together Books, an anarchist bookstore that is run by a collective and is directly tied to the grassroots nonprofit Prisoners Literature Project, which donates free books to incarcerated people.

Libraries are also a fantastic place to consume books. In addition to being a place to borrow books, libraries often house important community programs. This means that supporting your local library may also be supporting things like free internet or vocational classes for those who otherwise cannot access these resources. Libraries have come a long way in the digital age. Many libraries can help you borrow books from other networks they're connected with, dramatically expanding their offerings.

Also, e-books and audiobooks are available to borrow for free from many libraries with apps like Libby. You can even borrow graphic novels from your library and read them on your Kindle, which can help you zoom in on panels and text.

Use the space below to write down some independent local and online bookstores that you can patronize and signal-boost to others. Also, write down the location of your nearest library and identify at least one community event or resource you can signal-boost:

_____

_____

_____

_____

Comic book stores are like the Fortress of Solitude for us nerds. Even with all of the online options out there, sometimes you just want to hold that graphic novel or comic in your hands in a quiet, restorative environment. Comicshoplocator.com can help you find a nearby store. Like brick-and-mortar bookstores, comic book stores may also contribute directly to communities or causes that you care about.

Use this space to write down some comic book stores near you or online that you can patronize and signal-boost to others:

_____

_____

_____

CORPORATE AND FOR-PROFIT INITIATIVES

Queer Eye cohost Karamo Brown became known for his statement T-shirts in support of Black Lives Matter. After fans started asking where they could purchase T-shirts with slogans like "Black History Is More Than Slavery," "My Brown Skin Should Not Be Feared," and "Sandra Atatiana Breonna #SayHerName," Brown partnered with retailer Stands to raise money for the NAACP's Legal Defense Fund and True Colors United. True Colors United was founded by pop star Cyndi Lauper and works to support LGBTQIA+ people experiencing homelessness. The campaign coincided with the release of Season 6 of *Queer Eye*, and shirts sold out in just a few days.

Stands partners with celebrities including Wil Wheaton, Felicia Day, and Michael Sheen to sell unique fandom-based products, from T-shirts to jewelry, in order to raise money for specific charitable organizations. It also invites and employs fan artists to design its merchandise. While specific donation amounts are not disclosed, many of the campaigns donate 100 percent of profits after costs.

DONATION MATCHING

If you work for a large company in the United States, your organization may participate in donation matching. Some companies will match individual donations on a 1:1 basis, but others will match 2:1 or 3:1, up to a certain amount. There are limits on which organizations qualify for donation matching, but most nonprofits and educational institutions are eligible. Of course, companies do this because they can claim a tax exemption and because it gets them good press. Given what we shared about rainbow capitalism, it's okay to be skeptical about a corporation's motives in doing this. That said, a charitable organization may receive a more significant donation with corporate matching, and you may be able to claim the donation on your own individual tax return.

For more information on donating to charity and tax rules in the United States, check out www.usa.gov/donate-to-charity. This website also recommends researching the charity you are donating to by checking with the Better Business Bureau for complaints and with your state's attorney general for a list of licensed charitable organizations.

CONVENTIONS AND CONSUMPTION: PROS AND CONS

One of the most exciting (and expensive) parts of fandom is attending conventions. From huge, multi-fandom events like San Diego Comic-Con (SDCC), to smaller, fandom-specific cons held in community centers across the country, conventions bring in millions of dollars each year. Conventions also boost the emotional energy necessary for fan activism, as we discussed in chapter four. Celebrities may earn more from appearances at conventions than from their actual acting jobs! Photo opportunities (photo ops) and autographs (autos), on top of appearance fees, can generate huge profits. Conventions also help boost local economies by bringing in tourism and convention-adjacent spending. Plus, most companies pay significant taxes in order to host their events. Authors, artists, and creators who sell products at conventions also benefit from being able to sell directly to interested fan consumers. Basically, fan conventions are their own industry.

As a fan attending conventions, how you spend money has power. Choosing to attend a specific convention can be an opportunity to consider ethical consumerism. The biggest thing to consider when evaluating cons is whether the company that runs them is a nonprofit, like San Diego Comic-Con International (the organization that runs SDCC and WonderCon), or a for-profit. Organizations achieve nonprofit tax status when all the revenue made from the convention goes back into running and organizing it. Even if conventions are for-profit, however, they may feature charitable initiatives or include donations to nonprofit organizations. Denver Comic-Con was a local nonprofit convention that benefited Pop Culture Classroom, an organization that supports literacy through using popular culture in K–12 classrooms. After COVID-19 forced the cancellation of 2020's planned event, Denver Comic-Con was purchased by Fan Expo HQ and renamed Fan Expo Denver. Fan Expo HQ is a subsidiary of a multimedia conglomerate called Informa, but profits from Fan Expo Denver continue to support Pop Culture Classroom.

Creation Entertainment specializes in both official and unofficial show or product-specific conventions. Creation's main advantage, for official licensed events, is that it signs exclusive appearance deals with show stars and offers a smaller, show-specific experience for fans. The main disadvantage is that, because of this specialization, ticket prices can be much higher than at other cons. Notably, there are often charitable donation opportunities in the vendor rooms at Creation conventions.

Use the space below to write down some fan conventions near you, and then follow up to check if they are for-profit or nonprofit conventions:

When attending conventions, it's also important to consider the overall values of the organization putting the event together

Convention Name (and Dates)	For-Profit	Nonprofit

and whether those values align with yours. For example, many conventions work hard to ensure the safety of attendees and cosplayers. If you are considering attending a con or event, look for codes of conduct and signs indicating appropriate behavior, including norms about taking photos of cosplayers. Many conventions are becoming more explicit about anti-harassment policies. You might also ask yourself what else the organization is doing to support an inclusive, positive experience for fans. What kinds of panels, for example, is the convention including? Are there panels featuring BIPOC creators? Does the convention have family-friendly events and transgender-inclusive restrooms? What about inclusion of people with disabilities? Are spaces accessible for wheelchair users? Is ASL interpretation available for deaf fans? Even if you do not share these identities, as an ally, it's important to consider who is included in fan spaces and who is marginalized through "standard" practices.

BOYCOTTS AND DIVESTMENT CAMPAIGNS

Boycotts and divestment campaigns have been some of the most successful collective action strategies used by activists over the last few decades. Drawing on the power we have as consumers, boycotts work by asking people not to purchase, use, or patronize a store or corporation. The power in this strategy comes from being willing to go without a certain good or service in order to ask that the company or business providing said service change its practice. Notable boycotts in history have included the United Farm Workers boycott of American-produced grapes and lettuce, advocating for better labor standards, and the divestment, or disinvestment, campaigns targeting South African businesses in the 1980s to protest apartheid. One of the most impressive examples of fan activism was a boycott. Fandom Forward organized fans to protest the use of child labor in the production of chocolate for Harry Potter–themed candies, especially Chocolate Frogs. Warner Brothers committed to ensuring that all chocolate used would be fair trade certified by the end of 2015.

Fans are creative when it comes to expressing their dissatisfaction with a particular creator. In 2013, when a film adaptation of *Ender's Game* debuted, Geeks OUT organized a boycott, asking fans to publicly sign a pledge to skip the film. Geeks OUT is a nonprofit that works to support LGBTQIA+ rights, representation, and advocacy in the geek community.[20] Some fans—who loved the books but wanted to subvert supporting creator Orson Scott Card due to his homophobic views—purchased tickets to

20   For more on the Geeks OUT boycott, see: Todd Cunningham, "Ender's Game' Boycott Protests Author's Anti-Gay Marriage Stance," *The Wrap*, July 7, 2013, https://www.thewrap.com/enders-game-boycott-protests -authors-anti-gay-marriage-stance-101551/.

different films showing at the same cineplex and then snuck into the *Ender's Game* showing.

Boycotts can also help when it comes to issues of representation (or lack thereof) in media. The live-action adaptation of *Ghost in the Shell* (originally a Japanese manga and anime) bombed at the box office, perhaps in part because of the decision to cast a white actress in the lead role, which many interpreted as whitewashing. Whitewashing, the practice of casting white actors as characters of color, is nothing new. But the ability and willingness to call studios and production companies out on the practice is.

When news broke that M. Night Shyamalan was tapped to direct a live-action version of *Avatar: The Last Airbender*, fans were excited. In the original animated series, most characters, including the leads, are depicted as people of East Asian or Indigenous Inuit decent. The show is beloved in part because of its diversity in the representation of race, ethnicity, and disability. Fans were understandably frustrated when white actors were cast for all the main leads of the film. Fans upset with this casting decision organized a community on LiveJournal. Two fans in this community later organized a website called Racebending.com to address this and other media examples of casting white actors in roles originally depicted as people of color. (As a term, "racebending" is a play on the type of superpowers that *Avatar* characters have, where they can "bend" the elements of fire, water, air, and earth.) Through these online communities, fans organized information campaigns and petitions and handed out buttons and flyers at San Diego Comic-Con and other events. Fans against racebending encouraged writing letters of protest to Paramount Studios and director M. Night Shyamalan. Though one of the lead actors was recast with an actor of South Asian descent, it did not go unnoticed that all of the heroes were now white actors, and the one character with darker skin was the villain. Boycotts of the film helped tank the adaptation at the box office.

INVEST IN DIVERSE REPRESENTATION

Consumer practices can also influence what media representation looks like. We've discussed how boycotting and divesting can impact representation, but investment—making a point to spend money on good representation—can help, too. For example, increased diverse representation in MCU began to occur only after the box-office success of *Black Panther* proved that audiences would show up for stories about BIPOC heroes. *Black Panther*'s success paved the way for all manner of increased diverse representation in both the MCU and its spin-off television series.

SUPPORT DIVERSE STORYTELLERS

Better representation also happens when underrepresented people tell their own stories based on their lived experience of their identities. This is because those storytellers know things about their culture that others just don't—things that others might even get horribly, horribly wrong. As someone who participates in fandom, you've probably seen a caricature of yourself as a stereotypically childish, socially inept, and pathologically obsessive nerd or geek (think Comic Book Guy in *The Simpsons* or Annie Wilkes in Stephen King's *Misery*). Not how you would portray yourself if you were telling your own stories, right?

Supporting diverse storytellers also means engaging with media that tells stories different from your own experiences and identities. This doesn't mean you won't have anything to resonate with in a story told by people who are different from you—just that nuances of character experiences in the narrative will not be shared. *Squid Game*'s narrative may focus on many themes specific to Korean culture, but audiences outside of Korea have been able to find entertainment and meaning in the show's depiction of class inequality, poverty, and human connection. Furthermore, fan-made content about translation errors and culturally specific themes in the Netflix series has no doubt led to increased cross-cultural discourse and understanding. The popularity of the show has also sparked a great deal of conversation about the production and dissemination of media outside of the United States. In particular, it has challenged a Hollywood myth that English-speaking people will not read subtitles—something that has previously limited the audience of many films produced outside of the United States. After all, we don't question subtitles when Harry Potter uses parseltongue or when any number of characters in *Game of Thrones* speak in their native language, so why not consume other media in which subtitles are used?

Supporting diverse storytellers can also mean supporting other fans telling their own stories. You are supporting some of those stories by reading this very book, as it contains some of the authors' personal narratives. You can support content creators on various media platforms by liking, subscribing to, or sharing (with permission, if necessary) their content. You can even just share appreciation through comments and other forms of offering kudos. A kind comment can go a long way in encouraging someone to keep telling their stories, especially when underrepresented storytellers otherwise face a great deal of oppression. You can also do something as simple as suggesting diverse content to friends or encouraging cross-cultural consumption.

When was the last time you watched something that was totally outside of your media comfort zone—something written, directed, or acted by someone with a marginalized identity that you don't share? List one thing you can watch, read, or listen to that supports diverse storytelling and represents a community you do not personally belong to. List one person you can share it with:

I will watch, read, or listen to: _____

_____

I will share it with: _____

KNOWING WHAT GOOD REPRESENTATION LOOKS LIKE

Good representation is, to some degree, subjective because we will all feel individually represented by different things and in different ways. However, there have been attempts to standardize what good representation looks like. For example, you might have heard of the Bechdel test, a means of evaluating the representation of women in media, whereby good representation requires, at minimum, that there be at least two characters who are women, that the women talk to one another, and that the subject of conversation be about something other than a man. Similar tests have been created for other forms of representation in the media, such as the Vito Russo test for judging representation of LGBTQIA+ characters and the DuVernay test for judging BIPOC representation. While these tests and others like them can be a helpful place to start, it is important that they not be applied without attention to nuance. There are countless examples online, for instance, of movies with strong feminist themes that do not actually pass the Bechdel test.

Rather than rely purely on these tests of representation, another strategy would be to look at what marginalized communities are saying about how they are represented in various media. Often, their commentary will focus on potentially harmful tropes (that is, themes in storytelling) that either reinforce stereotypes or overrepresent only one aspect of identities, thus failing to capture the range of diverse experiences within otherwise marginalized communities. It is unlikely that you will find one singular perspective that will tell you if representation is good or bad because marginalized communities, like all communities, don't operate from a single perspective. Rather, taking the time to look at multiple critiques from different sources might illuminate aspects of a particular piece of media that you hadn't thought of before, even if you yourself belong to the group represented in it. Representation that includes multiple characters from a historically marginalized identity shows that no identity group is a monolith and helps avoid tokenization. This is part of what *Black Panther* does so well. As shared mythos, representation is just as much an ongoing conversation as it is a goal we should be striving toward.

Better representation can also come from subverting an expected narrative. For example, the *Watchmen* series centers around its Black characters by repeatedly subverting audience expectations about representation. The series opens with a film reel of a Black cowboy (a much more accurate historical depiction of a cowboy, but not what we are used to seeing). It then shifts to depictions of the real-world 1921 Tulsa Race Massacre, which saw white residents of Tulsa, Oklahoma, take the law into their own hands and lawlessly terrorize a Black neighborhood, leaving businesses destroyed and several dead. *Watchmen* shows us that protagonists aren't always white, and vigilantism isn't always justified. In fact, sometimes vigilantism is just white nationalism dressed up in a costume. These subversions of popular myth also allow *Watchmen* to successfully address real-world issues, like the Black community's fight for reparations, by showing us a world in which reparations did, in fact, happen. In other words, subverting the narrative, when the narrative has been lacking in representation, can be a powerful statement made simply by shifting the lens and key events through which the narrative is viewed.

CLIMATE CHANGE MITIGATION

Being conscientious about your consumption isn't just a moral thing to do; it's also important to consider how consumption affects climate change. Shopping local and secondhand can help reduce overall greenhouse gas emissions—the largest single factor causing climate change. Many of us came to rely on delivery more than ever during the initial shutdown of the COVID-19 pandemic to mitigate exposure. When possible, combine shipments into one delivery or one package to minimize fossil fuel use. Just like you'd try to run all of your errands in one trip to save gas (and time!), think about how your ordering practices could also change to be more sustainable. Many companies are now also offering a "carbon offset" option when you order delivery. For an additional fee, you can have the carbon cost of your delivery offset. Typically, this means the company you're purchasing from will donate the equivalent of your delivery "charge" on the environment, if you will, to a sustainable or renewable energy investment, such as wind or solar. Some companies are also up front about their investment in and use of renewable energy to produce their goods. In larger cities, many food delivery services use either bike or skateboard delivery to reduce driving and greenhouse gas emissions. Look for takeout options with eco-friendly containers and sustainable delivery methods when ordering.

SWAPS AND SECONDHAND SHOPPING

Landfills are the third leading contributor to human-produced methane gas. The more we can reduce our waste and keep things out of landfills, the more we can help mitigate this dangerous greenhouse gas. Freecycle.org is a nonprofit founded in 2003 that keeps items out of landfills and helps connect people with things they need or want. Craigslist and Nextdoor pages also have "free" sections. You may need to travel or arrange pickup of items, but these are pretty amazing services. You can post both requests and offers. Freecycle also includes borrowing or lending opportunities (for the once or twice a year that you need a specific tool) and a service called Friends Circle that allows you to select specific people to borrow, lend, and exchange with.

Think about fandom-related collections you have. Is there anything you might want to swap or donate? Maybe you've moved on from your Pokémon obsession and there's a seven-year-old out there who would love some gently used cards. Are there specific items you are looking to add to your collection? Write down a few of those, too. Who knows? You might luck out and find a great trade!

Use the space below to write down or take an inventory of fandom merch you might want to swap or donate:

_____

_____

_____

_____

_____

Use this space to write down items you would like to add to your collection:

_____

_____

_____

_____

_____

"DON'T CROP PHOTO OPS!": NON-TANGIBLE CONSUMPTION

Fans are amazingly creative when it comes to engaging with their beloved content. Cosplay, fan fiction, fan art, videos, livestreaming, memes, and photos are just some of the myriad ways fans explore and engage in fandom. Consumption in fandom often includes reading, viewing, or listening to these non-tangibles. Often, this consumption also involves sharing or resharing the fan works on social media sites. And while this is a good thing—we all get a kick out of friends sharing clever and fun images with us—recently, some have been sharing others' work without giving credit to the original creator.

Although social media has been a part of our lives for the better part of twenty years, norms around how we communicate and share things are still evolving. Many of us have shared without crediting the original source. But this is bad form; it's important to try and find the original creator and give credit where it is due. With respect to sharing photo ops, fan art, memes, or other fan works on social media, the norms are pretty clear: don't share without permission or post to other sites without permission, don't crop out a creator's name/logo/watermark, and credit the original artist/maker. This is especially concerning when it comes to photo ops and privacy violations for minors. Just as you'd ask for a photo of a cosplayer and for explicit permission to share said photo, especially if the cosplayer is a minor, ask if you can share any photo ops you come across. Even if a fan shares a photo-op image in a fan-based group page, be sure to request permission before sharing it elsewhere.

INTELLECTUAL PROPERTY ISSUES

Fandoms coalesce around intellectual properties. The stories, images, and media that we connect with and use to express ourselves are someone's brainchild. Sometimes the line between fair use of copyrighted content and theft is a blurry one. Typically, transformative works like fan fiction or fan art are not considered copyright infringement under fair use laws.[21] When it comes to ethical consumption of fandom consumer goods, however, it can feel like trying to navigate through the Misty Mountains!

Try to use your best judgment when considering the type of merchandise you are buying. When purchasing mainstream fandom paraphernalia—like a *Star Wars* T-shirt, for example—it's best to stick with officially licensed products. You can usually tell if something is officially licensed by carefully looking over the item listing or packaging. When it comes to more transformative fandom-related content or fan art, things can get a little trickier. Because fan art references someone else's intellectual property that is often protected by copyright, fair use can become a gray area. If a small, independent creator is not making a large profit from their work or is referencing the source material without exactly copying the symbols or logos, most large corporations will overlook the production. For example, let's say an independent creator draws a Captain America–inspired fabric pattern that is

21   For more information on transformative works and fair use, see: "Fanworks, Fair Use, and Fair Dealing," Organization for Transformative Works, accessed June 3, 2022, https://www.transformativeworks.org/fanworks-fair-use-and-fair-dealing/.

then used to make leggings or dresses sold at conventions. As long as they are not trying to sell that product as official Captain America apparel or using language or logos that are too similar to that of the source material, they are typically left alone.

Theft of intellectual property does happen, however. When retailer Stands partners with celebrities to sell fandom-inspired T-shirts that raise money for charity, the designs are often stolen by other sites and sold for much less than the original price. When purchasing a fandom item, verify that the design was not stolen from an independent artist. One strategy is to do a quick Google image search before purchasing. If possible, it helps to try and find where the original design came from and maximize the money going to independent artists or official merchandise.

SOCIAL MEDIA AND PEOPLE AS PRODUCTS

Social media is critical to a lot of activist strategies and can be exploited for good. But the truth of the matter is that if you are on social media, you and your use of those platforms are products being sold to advertisers. If you are the product, however, then you can brand yourself—something big and small users of social media alike do to draw attention to particular causes or to raise money.

An excellent example of people as products is social media influencers who monetize themselves as brands via various forms of sponsorship. Many influencers raise money or awareness about causes, and some even build their personal brands around a particular cause. Another example of people as products is OnlyFans. Though the site is best known for its adult content creators, it is, broadly, a pay-per-view platform through which independent creators develop a fandom based around their content. Some content creators have specifically built their brand around activism, using the pay-per-view feature to generate revenue for a particular cause. This is similar to how celebrities and Starticipants sometimes build a public persona around a particular form of activism. We all associate Leonardo DiCaprio with environmentalism due to his appearances in films like *Before the Flood* and *Don't Look Up*. OnlyFans creators, however, don't need to have a lot of existing monetary resources to promote themselves in the same way that a celebrity does in order to make or star in a film.

OnlyFans also provides a great example of how people as products can contribute to larger social movements when they and their fandom stand together. In the summer of 2021, the website moved to effectively ban adult content. This caused a flood of creator and fan activism, which ultimately resulted in a reversal of that decision. Not only was this a win for those particular creators and their fans, but it also drew larger attention to sex workers' rights movements as a whole. Similar people-as-products-promoting activism can be found on platforms like Cameo, where you can purchase personalized recorded messages from activists who have their own fandom following as a way to sustain their work.

You don't have to create content, per se, or have your own following to have some sway on social media. Even just developing an online persona around activism can pique the interest of others. For example, if you are someone who posts a lot about Black Lives Matter, you may become known to your followers as someone with whom others can talk openly about anti-racism. You can also use your online network to your advantage to get more eyes on a fundraiser, or even to start a fundraising effort of your own.

Considering what you consume and how you consume it can be an excellent gateway into fan activism. Ensuring that the media and products you consume align with your values will help support a more equitable and inclusive community. There is power in voting with your dollars and attention. After all, without fans, there's no market for genre media and products!

Chapter 7

YOU CAN'T POUR FROM AN EMPTY CUP

"Sleep is a curse, and yet a curse I need to live."
Steven Universe, *Steven Universe* Season 2, episode 10

WHAT IS SELF-CARE?

Engaging in activism can be physically and emotionally draining. When you care about the work deeply, you'll probably also feel like there is always more to do—and that you need to do it all. It is critical, however, to recognize your limitations and take breaks to rest. When you hear the word "self-care," you might think of social media posts about how spending money on massages, pedicures, or flashy vacation getaways is totally worth it. But doing anything you have to do in order to be emotionally and/or physically available for activist work is self-care. Self-care can be as simple as taking the time to breathe, sleep, eat, and anything else your meat-suit needs to keep going. If you are resourced enough to get massages and pedicures or to go on vacations, it can mean that, too. It just doesn't *have* to be that.

THIS IS A TEAM EFFORT

The first key to self-care is remembering that you are part of a team. No one is responsible for carrying the weight of this work alone, and everyone has different strengths. Samwise couldn't carry the One Ring, but he could carry Frodo. Xander didn't have powers like the rest of the Scooby-Gang did, but that allowed him to see things others couldn't. Hawkeye was just a guy with a bow and arrow in a war against robots flying around a flying city, but he was responsible for getting a Chaos Magic–powered Wanda back in the fight. Sometimes we have to be the less-than-superhuman hero in activism. Sometimes we have to be Hawkeye.

Now, unless you are a huge Clint Barton fan, you are probably saying to yourself, "But I don't want to be Hawkeye!" Understandable. He doesn't have the impressive tech of Iron Man, the thunderous command of the sky like Thor, or the Super Soldier strength of Captain America. He was absent from *Infinity War*! We know, we know, but hear us out—there is no *Endgame*, no Thanos-defeating mega-battle, without Hawkeye. Yes, he takes breaks throughout the MCU films, but he always shows up when needed. He provides a safe house for all the Avengers, he comes out of retirement to stand with Captain America in protesting the Sokovia Accords, and he is recruited again to participate in the Time Heist. Not only is his presence necessary to retrieve the Soul Stone from Vormir, but he also ensures the safety of the Nano Gauntlet, used to reverse the Snap, by knowing his limitations and passing off the gauntlet to others at the optimal time.

Your task in activist work is to know when to metaphorically retire to your own safe house, whatever that might look like for you, and when to pass the gauntlet to other members of your team.

HARNESSING THE BALANCE OF POWER

There is a popular saying that "you can't pour from an empty cup"—or, if you're Hawkeye, "you can't shoot from an empty quiver," meaning that you are less effective if you are out of energy from doing too much. One way to stay energized is to balance work with self-care. The Infinity Stones also rely on balance, especially when they're all placed in the Infinity Gauntlet. If you are to wield the power of the Infinity Stones, you must do so through the mastery of opposing forces. You can only wield the power of time through the mastery of space, or the power of mind through the mastery of soul, and so on. Let's explore how you can use these principles to find balance in yourself to power up for your activist work. Below is a breakdown of each Infinity Stone: the power it grants, what it is powered by (i.e., what opposing force must be mastered to wield it), and what self-care strategies can be used to master that opposing force.

HOW TO MASTER TIME TO ACCESS THE MULTIVERSE AND ALTER REALITY (REALITY STONE)

It's easy to lose sight of the importance of taking time for yourself when you are focused on the collective good. Taking time to ground yourself will alter your reality by making it more tolerable. To do this, it may help to schedule breaks in your day, so create a routine that includes breaks for naps, yoga, mindfulness, and/or deep breaths. You can set reminders for yourself or

BALANCING SELF-CARE: WIELDING THE POWER OF THE INFINITY STONES

	Reality Stone	Soul Stone	Mind Stone	Time Stone	Space Stone	Power Stone
Powered Granted by the Stone	Access to multiverse / ability to alter reality	Manipulation of the soul/ resurrection	Telepathy/ intelligence/ mind control	Time travel	Teleportation	Physical power
Opposing Force That Must Be Mastered to Access the Power of the Stone	Mastery of time	Mastery of reality	Mastery of soul	Mastery of space	Mastery of power	Mastery of mind
Self-Care Strategy for Mastering Opposing Force	Take time for yourself, to ground	Feel your feelings	Balance action and inaction	Take up space	Speak up when you are burning out	Quiet your mind by focusing on the present

enlist someone in your life to help you stay on top of a particular self-care practice. If you take time to nap, make sure you are napping in a way that is regenerative and not in a way that could interfere with your sleep cycle. Most sleep scientists recommend limiting naps to thirty minutes or less and making sure that they do not occur too close to the time you usually go to sleep. If you do yoga or engage in another type of physical practice, consider regularly attending a formal class or setting regular days and times to practice. If you practice mindfulness, try practicing at the same time every day.

Mindfulness is a particularly helpful practice in grounding yourself because it can be done anywhere, doesn't cost anything, and can sometimes give you helpful insights into your care of yourself or your activist work. If you've never practiced mindfulness before, it's really just about attending to the present moment. Many mindfulness practices start with paying attention to your breathing because it's something we all do and can easily observe, and our breathing can impact our experience of stress. When you are feeling stressed or anxious, your breathing will likely be more rapid and shallow. If you become aware of your breathing, however, you can also alter it by taking intentional deep breaths or by engaging in a breathing exercise, such as counting your inhales and exhales. Simply noticing your breathing will sometimes naturally slow it because doing so draws your attention away from any thoughts that are causing you distress.

Of course, breathing is not the only thing you can redirect your attention toward. You can redirect your attention to any of the five senses (sight, smell, taste, touch, and hearing). You might take note of three to five things you can see in your immediate surroundings; notice the smells around you, or intentionally create a smell by performing an action such as lighting a candle; notice the way a particular food tastes if you eat it slowly; notice the way different objects around you feel to the touch; or notice the qualities of different sounds that occur in your home, in nature, or through something like music. If you don't like sitting still to do mindfulness (many people don't), you can practice it while also engaging in movement like walking, stretching, dancing, etc. There is no wrong way to engage in mindfulness because it's simply a matter of noticing things to bring yourself back to the present moment. You can also notice thoughts, feelings, memories, and behavioral urges. This can be a little more difficult, as our present-moment thoughts, feelings, triggered memories, and behavioral urges won't always feel pleasant. If you've never done any of this before, you might consider reaching out to a mindfulness instructor or psychotherapist for assistance with developing a practice that best suits you. You can also find mindfulness resources in your mobile app store and online, including videos on platforms like YouTube. If you are new to mindfulness, be sure to review the sources of any mindfulness tools you find to make sure you are dealing with quality information. One way to ensure a source is reputable is to check if it is linked to a medical center or academic institution, like a medical school or university.

Write down one way you can practice mindfulness during your week. If you already have a mindfulness practice, write down anything you could do to strengthen that practice:

_____

_____

_____

_____

_____

HOW TO MASTER REALITY TO MANIPULATE THE SOUL AND GAIN THE ABILITY TO RESURRECT (SOUL STONE)

Feel your feelings. Your feelings are your reality. You may find that you want to change how you feel when your feelings are painful, but we can't just will away a feeling. Honoring your feelings allows you to heal your soul. By caring for your soul, you honor those who came before you, allowing you to carry on their work. Notice and name your feelings; notice what body sensations come up in response to feelings; let yourself laugh or cry when you feel like you need to.

This is not a therapy book. If feeling your feelings is something you have trouble with or that causes you increased distress, working with a qualified mental health provider is highly recommended. That said, we are all already living with feelings every day, even if we aren't always making the space to fully feel them. Honoring your feelings can be as simple as just naming a feeling that you are having. If you have trouble naming your feelings, you can use a feelings wheel, like the one at feelingswheel.com, to increase your vocabulary. You can also identify feelings as something visual, like a shape or color, or by using any other sense that is most accessible to you (e.g., naming a feeling as a particular texture or sound). Noticing body sensations that come up in response to feelings can also help you identify what you feel, as well as help you notice when a feeling is building. For example, many people tense their muscles when they feel stressed. If you notice that you are tensing a particular muscle in response to stress, you can intentionally relax that muscle or otherwise give yourself a break, which may lessen the intensity of your emotions or make them feel more tolerable when they are unpleasant. We can't always change our unpleasant emotions, but just recognizing them and the impact they have on our bodies can help us better understand and feel less distressed by them. When honoring your emotions, it is important not to place any kind of judgment on what you feel or how you react. The practice is simply to notice what is there. If you feel like crying, for example, it's okay to cry. If you feel like laughing, that's okay, too. If you want to maniacally laugh like a supervillain and cry at the same time, maybe be thoughtful about where you do it, but honestly, that's okay, too. Activist work is emotional work, and it's okay to feel our emotions.

A good example of why it is important to feel our feelings is Wanda Maximoff's arc in *WandaVision*. Wanda suppresses her grief so much that she not only further harms herself, but also harms an entire town. Similarly, Bucky in *The Falcon and the Winter Soldier* is only able to move past his guilt about his past deeds when he allows himself to really feel and accept it. Now, you are probably not an orphaned witch imbued with Chaos Magic or a one-hundred-plus-year-old Super Soldier who carried out horrific acts under Hydra's mind control, but you get the point. These characters had to feel and accept their emotions in order to heal their souls, which ultimately led to more heroic acts from both of them. Wanda in particular has to accept reality over the sitcom-clad facsimile she has created in order to move forward and do good in the world. While she sacrifices much, opening herself up to grief also opens her up to love. As Vision explains in a memory, "What is grief, if not love persevering?" Wanda cannot feel love if she does not feel grief, and she cannot become the Scarlet Witch if she does not accept her feelings, painful as they may be.

Write down the first emotion that comes to mind when you think of activism. How do you know you are feeling that emotion? What does it feel like in your body?

_____

_____

_____

_____

_____

HOW TO MASTER THE SOUL TO GAIN TELEPATHY, INTELLIGENCE, AND MIND CONTROL (MIND STONE)

Balance action and inaction. Caring for your soul means recognizing that your actions have limitations. Doing only what you can is wise. By doing only what you can—what you are good at—you are more able to change the minds of others. Practice stepping forward and stepping back; volunteer only for the things you have time to complete; volunteer for the tasks you are best suited for.

When you are engaging in meaningful work, it can feel like you have to participate in every opportunity and share in every space, especially early on when you are trying to establish your voice and purpose in a particular movement. Stepping forward and stepping back is a practice of observing your participation and stepping forward if you haven't spoken or volunteered in a while, but stepping back if you've spoken or volunteered a lot. This is an important practice in self-care because staying observant about your level of participation, and stepping back when you've already said or done a lot, can keep you from overworking and burning out. In spaces where you are showing up as an ally, it is also an important practice in making sure you aren't overstepping. For example, a white ally in a movement like Black Lives Matter should maintain a balance between stepping forward so that Black people are not always burdened with being the ones to advocate for their own rights and safety, and stepping back to make sure the movement still belongs to Black members of the movement. Think of it like running the starship *Enterprise*. A ship that size can't function without a whole team of people stepping forward and stepping back. A crew member might step forward to help where they usually don't if another member of the crew is incapacitated or otherwise busy, but they would also step back if they themselves are injured, need rest, or simply aren't as needed in a given situation. This keeps the whole ship up and running while also ensuring no one person on board burns out.

Volunteering only for the things you know you can complete is another way to balance action and inaction. Not only does this keep you from stepping forward and taking on too much, but it also ensures that important deadlines or details in the work are not missed due to the impossibility of juggling too many things. If you do find yourself at risk of missing important deadlines or details, you might ask for help and/or extensions of due dates where you can. It's often better to push something back than to do it poorly or overwork yourself to the point of no return. Volunteering for the tasks you are best suited for can help here because it ensures that you are doing the work you are most familiar with and can probably complete with the least amount of energy. That's not to say you won't expend a lot of energy or time on tasks just because you are good at them—just that you won't have to spend as much time or energy as you would if you were doing something entirely outside of your existing skill set. Learning new skills can be important and highly useful, but you'll want to balance that with understanding when you have the bandwidth to learn a new skill versus when you might not. Think about the LARPers who help out in *Hawkeye*. They have a specific set of skills from their experiences of LARPing and their jobs outside of LARPing that are extremely helpful in the final conflict, but none of them personally step up to battle Yelena or Fisk because it's not their role. They would just get in the way. Kate, on the other hand, is in a position to learn new skills. She has the time to talk with Clint to learn and plan before they move in on the various threats. She is able to do this because she is also building on an existing skill set that she has honed over time. Everyone in that series is playing to their strengths and balancing action with inaction . . . except maybe Jack. He's just excited to be in the right place at the right time with a sword. He's certainly playing to his strengths in his own way, but it's more pure chaotic energy than it is intentional balance. Still, even he allows himself to be removed from the fight when instructed.

List one way you can step forward and one way you can step back in your work as an activist:

_____

_____

_____

_____

_____

HOW TO MASTER SPACE TO TIME TRAVEL (TIME STONE)

Take up space. This means taking up space in your team to ask for and accept what you need from others. Accepting what you need will help you have more time for difficult work. More time equals more progress. Ask for accommodations you need; ask someone to help you with your work if you get stumped or overwhelmed; practice saying "yes" when someone offers you help; accept compliments when others tell you that you are doing good work in activist spaces.

It can feel embarrassing to ask for what you need. Many of us have had the experience of being told that our needs are unimportant and have been made to feel like a burden for asking for help. That is the nature of some of the oppressive social systems we fight against: they tell us that what we need isn't important. But sometimes asking for what you personally need is its own form of activism that can have far-reaching impacts on many others. For example, asking for more sustainable pay while working for a community-based organization can ensure that others in your position also get paid better, leading to an overall more sustainable workplace. Asking for a larger font to be used on a PowerPoint presentation can help others who also need assistance with visual materials. Advocating publicly or being transparent about advocacy, especially in leadership roles, can help everyone feel safer while also keeping you from burning out by making sure you have what you need to carry on in the work. If you don't know what you need—if you are simply overwhelmed, confused, or overworked—you can simply ask for help. Sometimes it's easier to figure something out with the help of others. If you aren't used to asking for help, you might even just practice saying "yes" when help is offered.

Taking up space can also mean accepting compliments from others about your activism. We don't participate in activism for accolades, but that doesn't mean accolades don't feel good. Being told you are doing something meaningful or doing something well, if you can internalize that praise, can be extremely regenerative. If you aren't someone who easily accepts compliments, the first step in practicing internalizing praise can just be to accept it without self-deprecation. If someone thanks you for something, try saying "You're welcome" instead of "No big deal." Allow yourself and your work to be of value. Think about the television series *Loki*. In it, our primary Loki variant is not used to hearing good things said about him. He is a villain, and that view of himself limits his own exploration of his powers and abilities. It is only after characters like Mobius begin to see more in him that he is able to tap into new powers and become the hero. Loki has always sought to take up space, but they were never the right spaces. That's why he constantly fails. Only when he begins to internalize some praise does he start to take up space in a more effective way that makes him the hero of his own story. Self-focus, rather than selfishness, is what's needed here. Being able to discern the difference between needed self-focus and selfishness is crucial.

List ways you can work on taking up space in a self-focused way:

_____

_____

_____

_____

_____

HOW TO MASTER POWER TO TELEPORT (SPACE STONE)

Speak up when you are burning out. Your experience and ability to communicate that experience is your power. When you speak or otherwise communicate your truth, you have the power to move through the world in more effective ways. The more effective you are, the more your cause teleports forward. Communicate to people when you are heading toward burnout; communicate to people what feelings are coming up for you in your activist work; communicate to people about your hopes and goals.

Communicating your truth may sound simple; after all, you are sharing something you are intimately familiar with (that is, your own experience). But effectively communicating your truth takes skill. This is because our truths can be tied up in painful emotions or can impact the emotions or work of others. For example, if your truth is that you feel angry about the way someone else is handling a particular task in an activist circle, speaking your truth can have a real impact on that other person. If you are trying to communicate that you are headed toward burnout, that implies someone else may need to do additional work. There is nothing wrong with communicating these kinds of things—communicating them can be mission critical—but there are more and less effective ways to do so. You wouldn't want to just run into a room full of fellow activists and shout tearfully, "I'm angry and burnt out," for instance. That, at the very least, is going to get you some weird looks in most spaces, unless it is explicitly invited.

When thinking about how to communicate something effectively, it can first be helpful to think about the impact your statement may have on the person or group you are trying to communicate with. This is not to say that another person or a group's feelings, needs, and experiences are more important than yours (spoiler alert: they are not—all feelings, needs, and experiences are important in different ways and to varying degrees, depending on the context). Rather, you are considering how others will best absorb what you have to communicate so that you are most likely to get your needs met. A lot of us get into activist work out of some sense of righteous anger or fear, and those emotions are important tools in our arsenal. We just want to make sure we are using those tools with an audience that can digest and reflect rather than divest and deflect. If you think that your audience is more likely to do the latter, you might consider ways to reword your communication so it can be better received. This doesn't always feel good. In fact, it can feel downright oppressive, especially if you belong to a group for whom the dismissal of real, justified anger and fear is the very thing your activism seeks to improve. This is about *effective* communication, though—not *painless* communication. Rewording is just one tactic. You can also try different forms of communication. Written communication, for example, provides the added benefit of time to edit and reflect on a response so that you can calculate how to respond in a way that is both effective and values driven. We can do that when communicating face-to-face as well, but the speed of processing has to be a lot quicker, so practicing effective communication in that way is inherently more difficult.

Communicating effectively is also about safety. There is a physical safety to be had in communication, of course; saying the wrong thing in the wrong place can lead to violence. But when communicating about burnout in activist spaces, it's usually more about psychological safety. Now, psychological safety does not mean that you don't experience painful emotions, but simply that you will not suffer undue consequences as a result of communicating your truth with people you trust. The private conversation that Natasha and Steve have at Natasha's desk in *Endgame* is an excellent example of two people who have established a sense of psychological safety with one another. The two are both feeling burnt out. Steve communicates his sense of hopelessness, and, in turn, Natasha communicates her reasons to maintain hope. Both are letting down their guard in this scene, communicating in a way that is fundamentally different from the way they communicate with the public, or even with their other teammates. They are able to do this because they have a history and because Steve offers an invitation that Natasha accepts. They speak with emotion, but neither is accusatory or cruel in any way toward the other. Neither is at risk of losing the respect of the other, and both will go back to the work without reservations about their ability to function as a team because moments like these ultimately bring them closer together through a sense of mutual understanding. *That* is psychological safety. They both feel difficult emotions as they communicate with one another, but their roles and friendship are not assumed to be at risk for doing so.

Write down some sentences you could use to communicate a difficult emotion to a fellow activist or leader. What do you think the impact would be? How will you know you have the psychological safety to use your sentence?

I would communicate: _____

_____

_____

_____

_____

The impact that will likely have on the person I communicate to is: _____

_____

_____

_____

_____

I will know it is psychologically safe to communicate my sentence if: _____

_____

_____

_____

_____

HOW TO MASTER THE MIND TO GAIN PHYSICAL POWER (POWER STONE)

Quiet your mind by giving yourself permission to understand only what you need to. It is easy to get caught up in "what ifs." "What if this plan fails?" "What if I'm not good enough?" "What if I'm the wrong person for this work?" Our minds are full of "what ifs," and since we can't actually see into the future to know if an "if" is true, "what ifs" just busy our minds in ways that can make us feel anxious or depressed. In other words, ruminating over "what ifs" powers you down. Your mind and body are linked. When you care for your mind by letting go of the "what ifs" and trust that you can only understand what you need to and what is presently available to you, you can build more strength in your body and your mind. Practice letting go of the things you can't control; remind yourself that you can't know or solve everything.

Quieting your mind doesn't mean getting rid of "what ifs" and other thoughts. It simply means refocusing your attention so that your thoughts quiet down. This can be accomplished through mindfulness practices like the ones discussed earlier, but it can also be accomplished by doing instead of dwelling. Take for example Sam Wilson in *The Falcon and the Winter Soldier*. Sam spends much of the series plagued with "what ifs"—what if he isn't as good as Steve Rogers was, what if America doesn't accept him as Steve's successor, etc. Sam doesn't quiet his "what ifs" through mindfulness. Instead, he quiets them by accepting that he may always question himself but can take up the Captain America mantle anyway. He doesn't need to understand everything about why Steve chose him for the job; he just needs to understand himself enough to know that it is something he wants to do—and so he does it.

Write some "what if" statements that get in the way of your activism. Then, write down something you can accept about your "what if" statements.

What if: _____

_____

_____

_____

_____

I can accept that: _____

_____

_____

_____

_____

INFINITY STONE MINDFULNESS EXERCISE

Several of the examples of balancing self-care above recommend utilizing mindfulness. Below is a mindfulness exercise that references each skill, which you can draw on in your self-care practice. If you practice yoga or related philosophies, you might have noticed that the Infinity Stones are the same colors as six of the seven chakras. The below exercise can be thought of as a chakra exercise if you ascribe to the presence of chakras, but you don't have to use it that way if you don't want to. If you do use it as a chakra meditation, the chakras will be as follows:

Root = Reality Stone
Sacral = Soul Stone
Solar Plexus = Mind Stone
Heart = Time Stone
Throat = Space Stone

Third Eye and Crown = Power Stone

In an effort to attend to the ways in which mindfulness exercises can sometimes be ableist, there are lots of options given throughout the script below for modifications. If you come across something, however, that you cannot do—for example, if you are unable to take in the visual information around you at the end of the exercise—you can either skip what doesn't work for you or modify the script in any way that you need. You know your own needs. Similarly, the script tries to consider places where affirmations might be challenging and provides multiple options there. If any part of the script is challenging in a way that causes you to feel emotionally triggered, you can skip that section or stop the exercise. This isn't therapy. Those who are newer to or unsure about practicing mindfulness may benefit from practicing something like this with a therapist or mindfulness instructor. Lots of mindfulness tools exist on the internet and elsewhere that are easily accessible to anyone, but therapists who are well versed in mindfulness can help instruct you in how to engage in the practice if you aren't sure—or, perhaps more importantly, they can help you if you notice any difficult thoughts or feelings come up during the exercise (or from anything in this book, really). Activism is hard! It's okay if you need some additional help.

Find a comfortable seated position. Some people like to sit cross-legged on the floor, or upright in a chair with their feet planted on the ground and palms facing up or down on their legs. Just find a position that feels best in your body. It's okay to lie down, but standing is not recommended because you might unconsciously buckle your knees during the practice and fall down. Some people like to close their eyes during mindfulness exercises, but if that doesn't feel comfortable or safe, you can pick a spot on the floor or the wall to focus your gaze on instead. You might be wondering how you are supposed to do either of those things *and* read this exercise (fair point). You can try to memorize the exercise, or you might find it helpful to record yourself reading it out loud so you can follow along that way. If you record yourself, try to make sure you read at a slow, even pace, and be sure to pause between paragraphs so you have time to focus on each mindful task.

Once you are comfortable, you are invited to notice your breathing. You don't need to take deep breaths or otherwise change your breathing in any way. Just simply notice what it feels like to breathe. Notice the rise and fall of your chest and abdomen, the temperature of the air flowing in and flowing out. Notice if you are breathing through your mouth, your nose, or both. Just simply notice everything you can about your breathing. If you have a condition that impacts your breathing in any way, or if you find that noticing body sensations makes you feel anxious, you can skip the body-based parts of this exercise and just focus on the affirmations.

Once you have noticed all that you would like to about your breathing, send your breath to the base of your spine and pelvis, noticing where you connect with the ground or chair. As you do this, call to mind the image of the Reality Stone, the glowing red gem that gives you access to the multiverse and the power to alter realities. To master this power, you must first master time. You have the right to take the time to be here, to slow down, and do this exercise. Say to yourself, "I have the right to take time for myself, to ground." Take some time to sit with self-affirming "I am" statements about your activism, like "I am an activist," or "I am a person who stands for social justice."

When you are ready, move your breath to your belly. As you do this, call to mind the image of the Soul Stone, the glowing orange gem that gives you access to the manipulation of the soul and the power of resurrection. To master this power, you must first master reality. You have the right to feel whatever feelings activism brings up for you. Say to yourself, "I have the right to feel." Take some time, without judgment, to sit with and name any feelings that might be coming up. Simply say to yourself, "I feel _____," and, "I have the right to feel _____."

When you are ready, move your breath to the space between your belly and your chest. As you do this, call to mind the image of the Mind Stone, the glowing yellow gem that gives you the powers of telepathy, intelligence, and mind control. To master this power, you must first master the soul. Say to yourself, "I have the right to take action, but caring for my soul means recognizing that my actions have limitations." Take some time to sit with affirmations about what you can do. Say to yourself, "I can do _____," or, "I do what I can."

When you are ready, move your breath up to your chest. As you do this, call to mind the image of the Time Stone, the glowing green gem that gives you the power of time travel. To master this power, you must first master space. Say to yourself, "I have the right to love myself, which means taking up space to ask for what I need." Take some time to sit with this right to be loved while taking up space. You might say to yourself, "I am loved," or "I can take up space." You might find it difficult to name feeling loved. Many of us get into activism because we feel hated for who we are. It might help to affirm that you are loved by your fellow activists or to think of love as being more like compassion or acceptance. If you would like, you can imagine sending love to someone else and giving that person permission to take up space. Sometimes it's easier to start with building love and compassion for someone else before we can affirm that right for ourselves. Simply notice what is easiest and most accessible for you, and take a moment to gently acknowledge that experience, whatever it is. *That* is acceptance, and acceptance is love.

When you are ready, move your breath to your throat. As you do this, call to mind the image of the Space Stone, the glowing blue gem that gives you access to the power of teleportation. To master this power, you must first gain mastery of power more broadly. You have the right to communicate your truth. Your truth is your power. Say to yourself, "I can communicate my truth." If you don't feel like you can communicate your truth for any reason, you can take a moment to revel in simply *being* your truth. Even just existing can be a radical act of communicating your truth.

When you are ready, move your breath to your head. If you are doing this as a chakra meditation, you will focus on your third eye—the space between your eyebrows—for the first set of affirmations (the right to see), and the crown, or top, of your head for the second set of affirmations (the right to understand). As you move your breath to your head, call to mind the image of the Power Stone, the glowing purple gem that gives you access to physical power. To master this power, you must first master the mind. You have the right to see and understand only what you need to. Say to yourself, "I see what I need to see," and, "I understand what I need to understand." You can personalize this to your activism if you would like. For example, you might say, "I see a path ahead in this work," or "I understand what I need to right now about this system I am trying to improve." What is important is that you remember you cannot see and know everything, and that is okay.

Starting from the crown of your head, send your breath back through your body, stopping briefly at each area you previously focused on to simply acknowledge the Stone you held there. You can imagine the light from the Stones dimming as you pass each one, or you can imagine putting them away into the Infinity Gauntlet. When you reach the end, say to yourself, "I have a right to all of these powers. This is me, and I am exactly as I need to be to wield the powers of the Stones for good."

With your best Iron Man snap, bring your awareness back to your breathing, and notice if anything feels restored. It's okay if it doesn't; just notice what it feels like to focus on your breath again, the same way you did at the beginning of the exercise. When you are ready, expand your awareness from your internal experience to your external experience. Notice your body in the room around you, perhaps by wiggling fingers, toes, or limbs. You can take a stretch if that feels good. If you've been closing your eyes, you can open them now. With your eyes open, take in the surrounding area. You may close this exercise with a breath, a sound, a stretch—really in any way you would like.

BUT WHAT IF YOU *ARE* SUPERHUMAN?

When you engage in activist work, you might start to feel super-human, especially if you can directly see the impacts of your own behavior on real-world change. Even superhumans need self-care, though, and to prove it, below are some examples from popular media that you can also apply to yourself.

The Original Avengers: Make time to eat. In the first *Avengers* film, there is an end-credits scene in which our heroes take a break to celebrate their accomplishments by eating shawarma, which not only helps them reenergize, but also supports a local restaurant that probably needs the business in the wake of the destruction caused by the Battle of New York. They also share the meal as a community, allowing them to bond together as they reenergize.

Wanda Maximoff: Stay hydrated, and have a cup of tea. At the end of *WandaVision*, Wanda has a pretty big task ahead of her: combing through the multiverse to find her kids using Chaos Magic. While doing so, she takes the time to relax and have a cup of tea. You don't have to literally split your consciousness into a separate apparition to do this, though. You can just take a break to hydrate before going back to your work.

Sam Wilson and Steve Rogers: Go for a run. While Sam has a tough time keeping up with Steve advancing on his left, the pair understands the importance of a good run. If running isn't your thing, you can walk, swim, bike, or enjoy any other activity that gets you moving.

Bucky Barnes: Go to therapy. He may not always heed the advice of his therapist, but Bucky eventually does the hard work of truly facing himself and finding a new path forward. The things that lead us into activism are sometimes traumatic. You don't have to deal with that trauma alone. If you like the techniques described earlier in this chapter about self-care, many of them stem from the philosophies and science behind therapies like Acceptance and Commitment Therapy (ACT) and Mindfulness-Based Stress Reduction (MBSR). There are also trauma-specific therapies you can seek, such as Cognitive Processing Therapy (CPT), Prolonged Exposure (PE), Dialectical Behavior Therapy Prolonged Exposure (DBT PE), Eye Movement Desensitization and Reprocessing (EMDR), Imagery Rehearsal Therapy for nightmares (IRT), Narrative Exposure Therapy (NET), Seeking Safety, and Skills Training in Affective and Interpersonal Regulation (STAIR). These are just some of the types of therapies available. A well-trained therapist can help you decide what therapy is right for you, even if it is not the specific therapy they are trained to provide (in which case they may give you a referral).

T'Challa: Lean on your communities for strength. T'Challa doesn't just get his strength from the Heart-Shaped Herb he consumes or from the vibranium in the suit he dons. The Black Panther draws his strengths from his ancestors and his community of Wakandans.

Rhodey: Seek medical attention when you need it! You probably won't get robotic, Stark-tech legs, but you are still likely to get some much-needed support and healing. Don't wait until you are critically injured. Preventative health is important, too, like making sure you get screened for curable ailments, getting vaccinated, etc. Preventative health won't protect you from accidentally getting shot out of the sky by Vision, but it will keep you otherwise battle ready.

FANDOM AS SELF-CARE

Engaging in fandom can itself be a form of self-care. Through fandom, we engage with like-minded others who support us for exactly who we are, and that can go a long way in helping us recharge or power up. Your version of a restful getaway, for example, might be an annual trip to your favorite Comic-Con or a monthly *D&D* night with friends. You probably engage in self-care without even knowing it!

INTENTIONAL USE OF FANDOM

Intentional use of fandom can be thought of as mindful use of fandom. Now, you might be thinking, "Isn't fandom and popular media kind of the opposite of mindfulness? Isn't mindfulness the quiet breathing thing I did earlier?" Remember, mindfulness is literally just being in contact with the present moment in a way where we don't judge ourselves or our experiences. The reason mindfulness is an act of self-care is that most painful feelings come from getting caught up in thoughts about the past or worries about the future. This can be especially true in activism, where the work can feel intensely personal and the stakes can feel incredibly high. Popular media often gets a bad rap in mindfulness circles because many people assume media consumption is inherently mindless. These people have clearly never met media fans! Research suggests that people who engage in fandom are anything but mindless in their consumption of popular media.

Rather, they are active participants, often recontextualizing or transforming the media. The level of attention and care fans take in their practice of fandom would knock most mindfulness practitioners right off their meditation pillows, if they only knew.

So how do you engage in mindfulness through fandom?

Gaming: Gaming can be a great way to engage in mindfulness. Most games are structurally similar to traditional mindfulness exercises. Like any good yoga class, games are specifically designed to hold your attention through brief, repetitive tasks that build on one another. The practice of mindfulness often relies on noticing when you become distracted and bringing your attention back to your point of focus. Games help you notice if you get distracted because distraction impacts gameplay. While often framed as a form of escapism, games can just be a different way to focus your attention.

Binge Watching: Have you ever watched your favorite show for hours on end, picking apart every little Easter egg, every hint of subtext, until you've totally reinterpreted what you just watched? Well, then you've mindfully watched that series. Mindful consumption of televised media means that you are tuning into the experience rather than tuning out of it, and no one tunes into series quite like serious fans who have a whole fandom to discuss their theories with.

Binge Reading or Listening: Much like watching televised media, reading books or listening to podcasts can be a mindful experience when one is fully tuned into the experience. The only difference is in which senses are most activated.

Mindful Creation: Whether you draw fan art, write fan fiction, or sew cosplay costumes, you've probably engaged in mindful creation. This is engaging in mindfulness through a creative process in which the repetitive skill you are building upon is the medium by which you are creating. You may notice the colors you are painting with, or you may notice the strokes of your computer keys or that one word you tend to use over and over in your writing. You may notice the feel of fabric in your hands while you sew or the temperature of your heat gun as you shape your foam body armor.

Mindful Engagement on Social Media: To mindfully engage in social media is to set an intention in your use of this tool. You are mindfully engaging when you notice what you are attending to and what you are not, as well as when you notice your reactions to posts and change your social media behaviors and settings accordingly to ensure a more connected experience. You might limit engagement with particular people or advertisements that trigger or stress you out. Similarly, you might follow pages and people that help you feel more grounded and uplifted. You might even connect with your inner truth through the art of memes.

Popular media, like anything else, is just a tool. It can be used mindlessly or mindfully; the choice is yours.

LEADING BY EXAMPLE

Fandoms themselves often promote self-care, including self-care while engaging in activism. GISH, for example, builds self-check-ins into its annual charity scavenger hunt, asking participants to make sure they are well rested and otherwise well cared for while they work to make the world a weirder and kinder place. During the 2020 US presidential election, Random Acts promoted #Snacks4Voters to encourage *Supernatural* fans to assist and uplift voters waiting in long voting lines to fulfill their civic duty. Also, many Starticipants post about their own self-care routines and generally advocate for mental and physical well-being through self-care.

While you may not be the leader of a movement—at least not yet—you can certainly lead by example through acts of self-care. One reason why it's so easy to forget to take care of ourselves in this work, and why it can be so easy to burn out, is that we don't always see examples like the ones above so clearly. We tend to see instead the strings of capitalism constantly pulling us to work harder and harder, even if capitalism is the very thing we are trying to undermine through our activism. Don't get caught up in that losing fight. Take care of yourself. We need you!

Chapter 8

THE DARK SIDE OF FANDOM

"A Jedi's strength flows from the Force. But beware of the dark side. Anger, fear, aggression; the dark side of the Force are they. Easily they flow, quick to join you in a fight. If once you start down the dark path, forever will it dominate your destiny, consume you it will ... A Jedi uses the Force for knowledge and defense, never for attack."
Yoda, *Star Wars: The Empire Strikes Back*

WHAT IS THE DARK SIDE OF FANDOM?

As absolutely amazing as fandom can be—as transformative and as much a force for good—like with all things, there can be a dark side. What constitutes darkness in fandom will be different for everyone based on how you participate in fan activities and relationships. The dark side of fandom consists of comments and behaviors that are mean spirited, bigoted, or contrary to your values as an activist. Sometimes the dark side presents as just one comment or behavior that impacts you or others in a deep and hurtful way. But it can also consist of many comments or behaviors that build up over time.

Acknowledging and addressing the dark sides of your fandoms can be its own form of activism, as this can sometimes bring about social change within fan culture. However, the main reason we've included this chapter is to help you identify potentially harmful things that can interfere with the longevity of your involvement with fandoms as social movements. Remember, fan activism is supposed to be fun! The dark side is the antithesis of fun.

FANDOM WANK

A lot of fan culture today exists in online spaces. While the internet can be used as an important tool for building community and engaging in activist work, it can also create problems. Fandom "wank" is one of them. "Wank" refers to online disputes that escalate from relatively small conflicts into significantly bigger conflicts within a fandom. The word "wank" stems from a Journalfen community that used to make fun of online conflicts in fandoms. Though the community no longer exists in its original form, the word is still sometimes used to describe this particular type of drama online. It is important, however, to distinguish wank from valid criticism, especially when said criticism is itself a form of activism.

Wank usually spreads online when fans escalate an issue by saying cruel things about one another in public forums. Activism, on the other hand, would be exhibited by anyone attempting to deconstruct or otherwise address the impact of a particular concern on marginalized communities, especially when said deconstruction is less personalized. Wank is, simply put, drama for drama's sake.

If you encounter wank, it's usually best not to directly engage, as drama for the sake of drama just wants to pull in more drama to keep the spectacle going. Sometimes you can more meaningfully comment by taking a step back and critiquing outside of the source of the initial conflict. For example, instead of engaging directly with wank on social media, you could comment on an instance of wank via a blog, submit commentary to a news source, or even submit a critique to an academic journal on fandom or communications. The benefit of stepping outside of the original source of the conflict is that you won't directly contribute to the drama. This means you can avoid proliferating the wank while still keeping meaningful conversations about the subject matter going. You can also support those who engage appropriately and/or indirectly, as they might be accused of fueling wank when they actually aren't. For example, if you see a BIPOC fan being accused of wank for making a valid criticism about the treatment of BIPOC fans within fandom, consider backing them up.

When you encounter potential wank, it can also be helpful to reach out to others outside your fandom to gain some perspective. The reason that wank spreads online is that the origins of an argument can get distorted and blown out of proportion. It's sort of like playing a game of telephone. If you've never played the game before, it starts off with one person whispering a message to another, and then that message gets whispered, one by one, down a line of people, with the last person in the line having to recite it aloud. The end message is usually a gross distortion of the original because the details get warped depending on what is heard by each person as they pass the message along. The internet can be like a giant, fast-moving game of telephone, where the origin of a thing gets broken apart and distorted or is influenced by the emotional reactions that people have when reposting about it. While emotional reactions are totally valid (we all feel what we feel, and that's okay—good, even), it's easy for one person's emotional reaction to influence the ways someone else reads about an event or situation. This is especially true if the emotional aspects of a repost are more obvious than the facts.

SHIPPING WARS

Shipping wars are a type of fandom conflict, occurring in person or online, in which two or more canonical or noncanonical character relationships are pitted against one another, or in which a specific relationship between characters is invalidated. Shipping is a common practice in most fandoms, with all types of romantic and sexual orientations explored by fans. Due to limited representation of LGBTQIA+ relationships in most media canon, shipping can be particularly important to sexual- and gender-minority fans as a form of representation or social commentary that can be achieved through fandom in ways it cannot (or just *is* not) in popular media. Shipping wars can be hurtful to fans because they can be interpreted as invalidating one's identity as a fan. They can also be experienced as dismissive or intolerant of a fan's own corresponding sexual or gender identity.

It's important when you see a shipping war to first evaluate the seriousness of the battle you are potentially sailing into. Some things that look like shipping wars might be more like military games—harmless sparring for the sake of sparring that isn't really hurting anyone. An example of a low-stakes war would be fans debating who the real OTP (one true pairing) of a franchise is without getting mean spirited about it (e.g., no name-calling and nothing too derogatory being said about any one ship). That kind of skirmish probably doesn't require any kind of intervention; it's just friendly debate. A more concerning shipping war is one in which fans of a ship are actively being slammed by other fans for pairing characters together. These are usually easy to spot because they feel like stumbling into an asteroid field. They seem fraught with danger, with little to no chance of escaping unscathed.

As a side note, while discourse on shipping does often refer to "pairings," that in itself is a little problematic because it excludes nonmonogamous ships. It's also important to note that not all shipping is sexual or romantic in nature. Asexual and aromantic examples of shipping also exist and are valid.

CYBERBULLYING

Cyberbullying is any kind of oppression, intimidation, or torment that occurs online. In fandom, cyberbullying can be enacted in both fandom wank and shipping wars, but it isn't exclusive to them. Bullying that occurs on the internet might involve the use of online tools, such as hashtags, which draw attention to a particular person or group. Notably, these tools can often be used positively as a form of activism, such as in the case of hashtag flooding, which involves fans co-opting the visibility of a hashtag by using it for something other than its intended purpose. K-pop fans have done this repeatedly, flooding hashtags related to hate speech with more positive words and images in an effort to reduce the visibility of the kinds of bigotry originally intended by the hashtag creators. This is still the internet, however, so it's important to attend to the ways in which activism like this may result in backlash from other fans who are not allies. Amber Miley does an excellent job of breaking this down in a 2020 article for K-pop news source *The Kraze*. In it, Miley shares screenshots of real examples of bullying within fandom and shares tips for boosting internet safety.[22] Some of these measures include the use of VPN protections to prevent against doxing and the use of within-platform tools on social media websites, such as use of privacy settings and disabling comments, to create additional layers of safety and privacy where needed.

---

22   For more on this, see: Amber Miley's article "Stop Pretending We Are All Nice People: The Dark Side of Being a K-Pop Fan," in *The Kraze*, June 27, 2020, retrieved from: https://thekrazemag.com/latest-updates/2020/6/27/stop-pretending-we-are-all-nice-people-the-dark-side-of-being-a-k-pop-fan?rq=bullying

Engaging online can be tricky because online spaces often carry some level of anonymity, meaning it can be difficult to know how much of an impact you are making when you enter an already-heated conversation, even with the best intentions. After all, some of the people you engage with might not even have real skin in the game. They could just be trolling. Before adding to comments online, you should ask yourself if what you are doing is really helping or if you are just poking a troll under the digital bridge. In other words, are you having a meaningful debate where you and others are effortfully considering one another's views, or are you just sort of yelling back and forth into the void? The former is a kind of activism; the latter is just frustrating.

OPPRESSIVE NORMS

Like with all cultures, a unifying factor of fandoms is the norms, or social rules, that fans follow and enforce with one another. There are formal norms, like written rules of engagement in online forums or rules posted at a convention for photo ops and autographs. There are also informal norms, such as knowing which kinds of questions are frowned upon by other fans at a convention or how to answer if someone asks, "Who shot first: Han or Greedo?" Informal rules are enforced not by law or authority but by other fans correcting behavior that falls out of alignment with the norm. Norms, however, can feel oppressive, especially to those who are marginalized by society at large.

If you encounter a norm that feels oppressive, you may be encountering a darker side of your fandom. Upon encountering such norms, it can be helpful to understand why the norm is there and why it is enforced. One of the best ways to challenge a norm that feels oppressive is to simply ask questions. If a norm doesn't hold up to questioning, it might be worth continuing to challenge it. This is particularly impactful when you question harmful jokes that reinforce norms. For example, if someone makes a sexist joke in your fandom, you could ask why it's funny or say something like, "Wait, I don't get it—what do you mean?" If someone has to explain a joke, it's probably not funny, and it causes the person who told the joke to reflect in order to explain it.

OTHERING

In activist work, especially if you belong to an oppressed or marginalized group, it's easy to see those who are outside your group as enemies instead of potential allies. This is also true of marginalized groups within fandoms. In sociology, this is referred to as "othering," and it can be related to the concept of minority stress. The theory of minority stress posits that people who belong to minoritized groups experience stressors like prejudice, discrimination, invalidation, or violence, which can lead to the internalization of those stressors as a form of self-preservation. One of the common ways those who experience minority stress will strive to protect themselves, consciously or unconsciously, is through hypervigilance and the development of negative expectations about the perceptions or future actions of others. This can lead to conflict and competition between marginalized groups where there could instead be alliances formed. We see something like this when we are first introduced to the Ewoks in *Return of the Jedi*. Both the Rebels and the Ewoks mistake one another for enemies at first. This makes sense, as both groups have repeatedly been made victims by the fascist Empire. They've been conditioned to assume the worst of one another to maintain safety.

Like for the Ewoks, attacks by one group toward another can also occur due to fear of losing power or territory that has been hard fought and won. That doesn't excuse attacks, but noticing this when it is happening can be the building block of allyship if both groups can recognize that the real enemy is the bigger entity that is doing them harm. The Rebels and the Ewoks are far more effective in bringing down the Empire together when they realize the oppressive regime is the real threat to them both.

USE THE FORCE TO DEFEAT THE DARK SIDE

While the above examples are a helpful place to start, the darker elements of fandom don't always brandish glowing red lightsabers that make for easy identification of their Force alignment. Just as some visions can be too vague to be immediately understood, many situations require some level of introspection and interpretation before action can be taken, because real-life situations can also be vague, with many interpretations depending on perspective and context.

In order to do this, you'll need to use the FORCE! Not the literal Force, but the handy acronym below, which will help you identify and respond to darker entities in fandom.

Feel: Identify your feelings. What emotions are coming up in response to a situation? Are any of these emotions paths to the dark side, such as fear, anger, or hate?

Observe: Identify the facts. What has actually happened? Imagine you are a droid interpreting data. Identify only objective elements of the situation.

Relate: Identify relationships that are impacted. Do you know anyone involved in the situation personally? How close are you to those people? What impact could action or inaction have on those relationships?

Contextualize: Identify any important context. Are there social or cultural factors that could alter the meaning of a situation?

Enact: Enact a plan to address the situation. Your plan should consider the intersections of feelings, observations, relationships, and context. How will your plan impact each?

The following fictional vignettes explore different examples of dark-side behavior in fandom. Read through each, using the FORCE to explore your reactions and possible responses.

Scenario 1: You are sitting at a convention. A fan, who appears nervous, walks up to the microphone to ask a question of the celebrity onstage. The fan starts by identifying themselves as a member of a marginalized community and begins to ask a related question about the actor's interpretation of a particular character's identity. Convention staff cut them off and escort them away from the stage. Following this, social media is abuzz with interpretations of what happened, both from convention attendees and those who were not actually there. Many fans suggest that an unspoken rule was broken, but they don't exactly give out manuals on unspoken rules, so it is unclear if the fan asking the question actually knew of such a rule. You weren't at the convention, but you see the conversation online and start to feel uncomfortable, as it is heading in a direction that seems really disparaging of a particular group of fans. Some fans, however, point out that the unspoken rule seems outdated and problematic.

Feel (identify your feelings): _____

_____

_____

Observe (identify the facts): _____

_____

_____

Relate (identify relationships that are impacted): _____

_____

_____

Contextualize (identify any important context): _____

_____

_____

Enact (enact a plan): _____

_____

_____

Scenario 2: One of your favorite actors from a show is doing a Q&A on a social media platform. Following a question about the show, the topic of shipping comes up. The actor appears flustered and makes some statements that sound, at best, ill informed, and at worst, heterosexist. You really like this actor and the character they play, but you feel uncomfortable with what has been said. You notice that some fans in the comments on the livestream are really upset, while others are making comments in support of the actor's statements. After the Q&A, your news feed is filled with commentary in which fans appear to be arguing about different ships in the show. One is a ship that is really important to you, one that you have written a lot of fan fiction about. The comments say mean things about people who like this particular ship. You notice a fellow author of fanfic that you follow trying to explain why the ship is important for diversifying representation in television.

Feel (identify your feelings): _____

_____

_____

Observe (identify the facts): _____

_____

_____

Relate (identify relationships that are impacted): _____

_____

_____

Contextualize (identify any important context): _____

_____

_____

Enact (enact a plan): _____

_____

_____

Scenario 3: Your favorite show just killed off a major character who embodied a marginalized identity. Characters get killed off on this show all the time, but this character is really important to fans who share this marginalized identity, and this isn't the first character with this identity to be killed off in order to move the plot forward for characters with less marginalized identities. Many fans are devastated, especially when they see that the show's network is participating in a diversity event using the character's image a week later. Those fans pull together a petition asking the network to address concerns about how representation is being handled. You notice that other fans online are making fun of the fans who are upset, and a related hashtag is trending.

Feel (identify your feelings): _____

_____

_____

Observe (identify the facts): _____

_____

_____

Relate (identify relationships that are impacted): _____

_____

_____

Contextualize (identify any important context): _____

_____

_____

Enact (enact a plan): _____

_____

_____

Are there any situations like these that you have experienced personally? Use the space that follows to work through some dark sides of fandom you have experienced firsthand:

Situation: _____

_____

_____

Feel (identify your feelings): _____

_____

_____

Observe (identify the facts): _____

_____

_____

Relate (identify relationships that are impacted): _____

_____

_____

Contextualize (identify any important context): _____

_____

_____

Enact (enact a plan): _____

_____

_____

Situation: _____

_____

_____

Feel (identify your feelings): _____

_____

_____

Observe (identify the facts): _____

_____

_____

Relate (identify relationships that are impacted): _____

_____

_____

Contextualize (identify any important context): _____

_____

_____

Enact (enact a plan): _____

_____

_____

Situation: _____

_____

_____

Feel (identify your feelings): _____

_____

_____

Observe (identify the facts): _____

_____

_____

Relate (identify relationships that are impacted): _____

_____

_____

Contextualize (identify any important context): _____

_____

_____

Enact (enact a plan): _____

_____

_____

SETTING BOUNDARIES

While it is important to enact plans to change the dark side of fandom when you can, it is also important to set boundaries around your participation in fandom and activism. Boundaries assert the limits that you can physically or psychologically withstand, and they are critical for maintaining balance between your well-being and your work. Examples of boundaries include putting space between yourself and an activity or person, ending a relationship or activity, or setting new rules about how you will engage with an activity or person. Let's use another acronym. To assert boundaries, let's work to master YODA.

Your feelings: Name how you feel.
Others' actions: Name the action that is prompting the boundary.
Describe the desired boundary: Name specific behaviors you would like to see changed.
Adapt boundaries: Renegotiate boundaries as needed.

Let's look at an example from the *Star Wars* franchise of mastering YODA to set boundaries. Ahsoka Tano asserts a pretty big boundary when she leaves the Jedi Order after being falsely accused of sedition in *Star Wars: The Clone Wars*. Below is that boundary, written out using the YODA acronym.

Your feelings: Name how you feel.

Ahsoka feels anger, betrayal, and doubt.

Others' actions: Name the action that is prompting the boundary.

Ahsoka was falsely accused of sedition, causing her to doubt the Jedi Council

and thus her own ability to belong to the Jedi Order.

Describe the desired boundary: Name specific behaviors you would like to see changed.

Ahsoka explains to the Council and her Jedi Master, Anakin, that she would

like to leave the Jedi Order and forge her own path. Anakin tries to stop her,

but she holds to her decision, noting that if the Council cannot trust her, she

cannot trust herself.

Adapt boundaries: Renegotiate boundaries as needed.

While Ahsoka does not return to the Jedi Order, she does continually

renegotiate her place in the fight against the dark side based on the

relationships she has with Rebels and former Jedi.

There is a valuable lesson about boundaries in Ahsoka's example: that, if you need to, it's okay to take a break or walk away from something you once held in high regard. If the dark side of fandom is draining your energy, it might be wise to separate from fandom momentarily or to change up your participation. For example, if you find yourself becoming upset about the posts you are seeing on social media, consider unfollowing or muting the sources of that distress. Alternatively, you could follow more people and organizations that better align with the type of participation that you find empowering. For in-person spaces like conventions, you might change up who you attend events with or what you do at those events. In some cases, you might even decide to leave a particular fandom altogether.

Now it's your turn. In the space below, practice setting your own boundaries based on any negative experiences you've had in fandom or activism.

Your feelings: Name how you feel.

_____

_____

Others' actions: Name the action that is prompting the boundary.

_____

_____

Describe the desired boundary: Name specific behaviors you would like to see changed.

_____

_____

Adapt boundaries: Renegotiate boundaries as needed. How might you be willing to adapt this boundary over time?

_____

_____

Your feelings: Name how you feel.

_____

_____

Others' actions: Name the action that is prompting the boundary.

_____

_____

Describe the desired boundary: Name specific behaviors you would like to see changed.

_____

_____

Adapt boundaries: Renegotiate boundaries as needed. How might you be willing to adapt this boundary over time?

_____

_____

Your feelings: Name how you feel.

_____

_____

Others' actions: Name the action that is prompting the boundary.

_____

_____

Describe the desired boundary: Name specific behaviors you would like to see changed.

_____

_____

Adapt boundaries: Renegotiate boundaries as needed. How might you be willing to adapt this boundary over time?

_____

_____

Sometimes new boundaries can be created collectively by fans who challenge a particular norm within a fandom. Some examples include creating new conventions that allow for types of fan participation marginalized elsewhere and the increasing presence of messaging at conventions that "cosplay does not equal consent" to touch cosplayers. In the case of creating new conventions, setting new boundaries involves the rejection of a previous boundary set forth by the majority fandom as well as the forging of new norms. In the case of messaging about cosplay and consent, setting boundaries is about stating that nonconsensual touching makes cosplayers feel unsafe and will no longer be tolerated.

Acceptance of what you as an individual can and cannot change is also a way of setting a boundary. This type of boundary is internal, and it's about deciding where to invest your time and energy. Acceptance does not mean you see the darker elements of fandom as justifiable or good, or that you never intervene. Rather, it means you accept that the dark and light exist together, and you acknowledge the limitations of your role. Just like we can't all be Hawkeye, we can't all be a Skywalker, either. Acceptance looks like shepherding yourself back to the *Millennium Falcon* while a Skywalker duels with a Sith Lord or Emperor Palpatine. You're acknowledging that there is something you can do in the situation, but that something isn't going to be taking down the biggest baddie in the universe all by yourself.

NAVIGATING PARASOCIAL RELATIONSHIPS

It's important to acknowledge that the dark side of fandom can also be driven by media creators and actors, not just by fans. This is important because, as we've discussed, we often develop parasocial relationships with these people or the characters they create and portray. As a reminder, parasocial relationships are best described as "sort-of" relationships in which we know more about a celebrity or character than they can possibly know about us. Despite the fact that parasocial relationships are, by nature, defined differently than the other types of relationships, they can *feel* just as important. For some fans, these relationships can even be an important part of personal identity development when fans draw conclusions about how to be in the world through the examples set by celebrities and media characters.

Like any relationship, parasocial relationships can go through breakups if a fan or fandom perceives the actions of the celebrity or character as being out of line. To be clear, we are talking about a metaphorical breakup that aligns with the parasocial nature of the fan/celebrity relationship. We are not saying that you or any other fans are secretly involved romantically with celebrities or fictional characters. That's not at all how parasocial relationships work. All that aside, research does suggest that parasocial breakups *feel* similar to other types of breakups, meaning their impacts and implications can be wide reaching depending on the intensity of how those relationships feel to fans. Even if you don't totally "break up" with a celebrity or character through your fandom, you might be greatly impacted by their words or actions if they are out of step with your values.

There is, of course, an important power imbalance to consider when navigating parasocial relationships. Celebrities, by way of being the people that we fan over, almost always have more power and less awareness of us individually within fandoms. This means that what they say and do can have a big impact on us, but it's unlikely a celebrity would be fully aware of that impact because they don't see each of our individual reactions. There may be some shared social space through conventions, online spaces, and other fan activities, but the balance of power and awareness is different than it is with people you have regular, ongoing conversations with. Though we recognize that there can be multidimensional parasocial relationships, in which celebrities and characters are inextricably linked, characters cannot respond back to fans without celebrity involvement.

So what do you do when a parasocial relationship is in turmoil?

DEATH OF THE AUTHOR

Many fandoms that have experienced a disruption in a once-beloved relationship with a creator have ascribed to something called "death of the author." This happens when all or part of a fandom collectively decides that a work is the property of the fandom itself and not of the problematic person who created it. When the author of the *Harry Potter* franchise released a series of tweets and other writings that were seen by fans as transphobic, memes appeared all over social media about how interesting it was that *Harry Potter* simply had no author. Some even jokingly suggested that actor Daniel Radcliffe, who played the lead role in the films, had penned the series himself as a young child. Everyone, especially fans, obviously knew that this was not the case, but the conversation was a way to separate the fandom from the creator. Fandom-led organizations like Fandom Forward distanced themselves by changing their name and released statements condemning the opinions expressed by the author. Activists suggested ways of engaging in the fandom that would not result in additional profits for the author, like buying used instead of new books or buying fan-made or secondhand merchandise.

Sometimes the author or artist is literally dead, and what feels problematic is a piece of media that hasn't aged well or newly uncovered information about an artist that does not paint them in a positive light. In the case of material that has not aged well, some fans point to historical relativism as a way to navigate their love of a now potentially problematic thing. Historical relativism is the idea that a piece of media can only really be understood in the historical context in which it was created—the material relies on its relationship to the narratives and norms that existed at the time of creation. Something that was revolutionary in the 1940s, for example, might not be so revolutionary today, and might even be viewed as problematic by today's standards. Take the debate of the popular Christmas song "Baby, It's Cold Outside." Many have criticized its lyrics in recent years for seeming to reflect the pressuring of women to give in to unwanted sexual advances, to the point that some have even rewritten the song to include new and more obviously consensual lyrics. Others, however, have pushed back, looking to the historical context in which the song was originally written—a historical context in which the woman's protests were perhaps not against her male companion but against the social norms of her time, which implied that she could not give the enthusiastic "yes" she wanted to give him and would need to keep up the appearance of saying "no" to not be judged by others for her own desires. Obviously, "no really means yes" is not the kind of clear, consensual messaging that we want to see in music today, but to say that the original song is implicative of rape culture also dismisses some important historical context.

When an author or artist is the subject of backlash more directly, death of the author becomes a little more literal in how it is applied. Death removes some of the cognitive dissonance one might experience as the result of fanning over a figure who is considered problematic because said figure no longer directly profits from the consumption of their art. Likewise, death removes the figure's ability to comment on potentially problematic behavior, meaning that accusations are more readily seen as speculation, as opposed to fact (assuming that anything controversial was largely uncovered post-mortem). There are numerous authors and artists across industries who have been accused at some point of problematic behavior, even criminal behavior, following their deaths, but there is less an attempt to "cancel" them, perhaps because death is already the ultimate cancellation. Instead, their work is often allowed to persist as part of the cultural zeitgeist in ways that the works of the living are sometimes not.

REDEFINING CONTEXT AND MEANING

The problem with "death of the author" is that many problematic creators continue to have a platform as a result of their initial popularity, even with the best of efforts by fans to reclaim a property as their own. This means that separating the work from the author doesn't stop the author from profiting or continuing to speak in ways we find reprehensible. Additionally, not all fans can fully separate a work from its creator because the actions of the creator sometimes feel too damaging. When fans cannot separate a work from its creator, another way to continue participating in fandom, and to keep loving the work, is by redefining the context in which you love something. This means redefining the meaning the work holds and what you feel most comfortable with moving forward.

We redefine context all of the time in fandom. For example, many people initially shipped Luke and Leia before learning they were siblings. That revelation caused us all, whether we shipped the characters or not, to recontextualize their relationship. We similarly had to recontextualize Darth Vader as a character when we learned that he was Luke's father. Recontextualizing your participation in fandom or your love of a work when there's a problematic author or other creative is very similar. You just take in the new information, process it, and decide what it means for your engagement moving forward. Recontextualizing can also be thought of as resolving cognitive dissonance.

Cognitive dissonance occurs when you receive new information that contradicts a belief that you hold. Hearing that a celebrity we love has said or done something we find objectionable causes dissonance between our beliefs about that celebrity before the transgression and after. Because that shift in perception doesn't feel good, especially for someone who may have put a lot of emotion and energy into being a fan of that celebrity, the reaction can be to justify or downplay the behavior. We all do this to some degree. Addressing cognitive dissonance isn't about never doing that, however—it's more about noticing when you might be doing it and questioning if there is something else you could try instead.

To address the cognitive dissonance caused by a problematic celebrity, you might continue to engage in fandom but not spend money that could directly profit a problematic figure. For example, you could wait to watch films until they are streaming, buy books only from used bookstores, or buy and trade merchandise secondhand. You might also decide that you love something for what it was when you first engaged with it and simply recognize that it's problematic now in the new context that surrounds it. When context changes, it's okay to stop loving something the same way as before. It's also okay to love what a work meant to you as a fan at a particular time in your life, while acknowledging that progress means wanting better from creators and other celebrities in the future.

CONSIDERING THE CREATIVES

Since parasocial relationships work both ways, it is not always an actor, creator, artist, or other fanned-over entity who is problematic. Sometimes it is the fans who are problematic toward these creatives. Many celebrities have suspended or permanently deleted their social media accounts due to online harassment. Kelly Marie Tran, for instance, has spoken publicly about the decision to leave social media following backlash about her performance as Rose in *Star Wars: The Last Jedi.* The backlash she faced was largely not about any kind of valid criticism concerning her character or her prowess as an actor; instead, it mostly consisted of remarks that were racist and sexist in nature. She was and still is supported by many fans who were eager for the kind of diversity that was ushered into the *Star Wars* franchise with the third trilogy, but fans alone were not able to police the massive amounts of vitriolic slander directed at Tran and other cast members of color. Tran was also supported by colleagues like Mark Hamill (Luke Skywalker), who condemned online tormentors of Tran via his own social media accounts. Activists can't win every battle, but it's important that we learn from examples like this and hold our communities to higher standards where we can, recognizing that we have as much a responsibility to diverse creatives as we have to diverse fans.

The dark side of fandom isn't always predictable, but it is, in some ways, inevitable. By staying grounded in your values, taking action, and finding acceptance in the things you do and do not have control over, you may be able to stay engaged in fandom in a way that is consistent with your activist goals. When actors and creators are involved, you may need to separate problematic people from their work or otherwise recontextualize and make new meaning with the information you're given.

Chapter 9

(CONCLUSION) TO BOLDLY GO

"Things are only impossible until they're not."
Captain Jean-Luc Picard, *Star Trek: The Next*
Generation **Season 1, episode 17**

From the earliest days of fandom, fans have been working together to fight for the greater good. In an era when political, social, and cultural divisions seem insurmountable, nerdy and geeky media may be the common ground that can bring us together. Through our research, we learned just how impressive fan activism can be. Fans, when united by a common goal, are truly magical!

You are now ready to embark on a journey into the world of fan activism. However, if you've ever completed a major goal or accomplishment—a college degree, a promotion at work, finishing a marathon—you know that achieving a goal often leads to new goals and new opportunities. This book can be your travel guide as you go forward, as well as a resource for inspiration and self-care. We don't know exactly where your journey will take you, but we do know it will change you and the world in unexpected ways. We hope we have encouraged you to boldly go into fan activism.

Finally, we leave you with a challenge: How will you answer the call to fight for inclusion and social justice? How can your love of fandom inspire you and help you realize positive change in your life, in the lives of those you love, and for people around the world? How can you join the heroic fight for chaotic good?

Activists . . . assemble!

RESOURCES

STARTING A NONPROFIT

Nolo

https://www.nolo.com/legal-encyclopedia/form-nonprofit-501c3-corporation-30228.html

Nolo has a number of online resources for small businesses, including nonprofits. The link above, however, will take you to a directory of information on filing a nonprofit name in all fifty states.

Nonprofit Ally

https://nonprofitally.com/start-a-nonprofit/

Nonprofit Ally has a broad array of content to help with setting up a nonprofit, including example bylaws. A lot of content is available without signing up for a membership, though both free and paid memberships are also available on the site.

NON-FANDOM-BASED ACTIVIST AND CHARITABLE ORGANIZATIONS

Habitat for Humanity

https://www.habitat.org/

Habitat for Humanity is a nonprofit organization that works to provide affordable housing options worldwide.

Doctors Without Borders

https://www.doctorswithoutborders.org/

Doctors Without Borders is an international organization that provides emergency medical and humanitarian assistance worldwide.

End the Backlog

https://www.endthebacklog.org/

End the Backlog is an initiative started by the Joyful Heart Foundation (https://www.joyfulheartfoundation.org/), a nonprofit organization that works to end sexual assault, child abuse, and domestic violence. Joyful Heart was founded by actor Mariska Hargitay (*Law & Order: Special Victims Unit*). End the Backlog works to raise awareness of the backlog on processing rape kits in the United States, as well as to ultimately increase processing on this backlog.

ETHICAL CONSUMPTION

Ethical Consumer

https://www.ethicalconsumer.org/

Ethical Consumer is a nonprofit organization founded in 1989 and based in Manchester, England. Its website contains free information and offers more detailed, customizable information on various industries for a fee. In addition to product and corporation information, Ethical Consumer includes information on active campaigns and boycotts and shares educational articles.

The Good Shopping Guide

https://thegoodshoppingguide.com/

The Good Shopping Guide is a UK-based organization funded by the sale of research and publications on ethical consumption. Since 2001, it has collected information on the ethics of over thirty thousand corporations. Its searchable database evaluates companies on a fifteen-point scale that includes assessment of environmental, fair labor, and animal rights practices. Corporations can pay to undergo ethical accreditation by the organization.

Green America

https://www.greenamerica.org/responsible-shopper

Green America was founded in 1982 and is dedicated to collecting and providing information on both environmentally sustainable consumption and socially responsible business practices. Recent articles include topics such as how to support Amazon warehouse workers and the costs of economic racism for Black Americans.

A subsection of this website, the National Green Pages, is a searchable database of socially responsible businesses: https://www.greenamerica.org/green-businesses-products-services.

Human Rights Campaign Corporate Equality Index

https://www.hrc.org/resources/corporate-equality-index

The Human Rights Campaign (HRC) is a large, nonpartisan advocacy and lobbying group based in the United States with the mission of ending LGBTQIA+ discrimination. The HRC has multiple tools on its website related to advocacy and education, including an annually updated Corporate Equality Index, which measures how well corporations treat LGBTQIA+ employees. With the popularity of Pride Month merchandising by corporations, sometimes called "rainbow capitalism," it's important to look at how corporations treat LGBTQIA+ employees to determine if they regularly stand behind a mission to protect and promote LGBTQIA+ people or if they simply slap a rainbow on some merchandise during June to make extra money.

Official Black Wall Street App

https://obws.com/

This app helps you find and connect with Black-owned businesses.

MULTI-FANDOM-BASED ORGANIZATIONS

Child's Play

https://www.childsplaycharity.org/

Child's Play is an organization that donates video games to hospitals and domestic violence shelters. According to its website, the organization was initially created as a way to give back while simultaneously challenging the false media narrative that video games are harmful.

Extra Life

https://extra-life.org

Extra Life is a fundraising program that benefits Children's Miracle Network Hospitals. Individuals or teams play games (both video and board games) to fund raise. To date, Extra Life gamers have raised over $100 USD to support children's health.

Fandom Charities Inc.

https://fandomcharities.org/

Fandom Charities Inc. is a nonprofit organization run entirely by volunteers that fundraises for various charities at fandom and media events.

Fandom Forward

https://fandomforward.org/

Fandom Forward (formerly The Harry Potter Alliance), or FF, is a fandom-based nonprofit organization that works to train young people to be activists. It works on a variety of issues, from water protection to LGBTQIA+ rights to supporting undocumented immigrants. The goal of FF is to make activism creative, joyful, and sustainable—very much in line with our goals for this book! FF has chapters all over the world; you can look at its website to see if there's one near you or if you are interested in starting your own chapter.

Gamers Outreach

https://gamersoutreach.org

Gamers Outreach is a non profit organization that works to provide video games and play opportunities for hospitalized children. From gaming as a fundraising option to direct donations that go to providing customized gaming consoles for hospitals, Gamers Outreach has raised millions to support children and their families.

GISH

https://www.gish.com/

GISH, formerly GISHWHES, stands for the Greatest International Scavenger Hunt. The hunt was started by Misha Collins in 2011 and runs annually. GISH is technically a for-profit organization, but its annual hunt and mini hunts have helped raise millions for charity and lead to countless hours of volunteerism all over the world.

Nerdfighteria and Project for Awesome

https://nerdfighteria.com/ and https://www.projectforawesome.com/

Nerdfighteria is the online hub for fans of all projects related to John and Hank Green, also known as the Vlogbrothers. Through this website, you can find out about local Nerdfighter groups who meet up for both social and charitable actions. Project for Awesome (P4A) is an annual YouTube-based telethon hosted by the Vlogbrothers where fans make videos in support of their favorite charities. To date, P4A has raised approximately $3 million for a variety of charities.

Parasol Patrol

https://parasolpatrol.org/

This Colorado-based organization seeks to protect LGBTQIA+ youth and their families from counterprotesters at events like drag queen story times and youth drag performances. Volunteers hold colorful umbrellas to shield the kids from hate speech and signs. Parasol Patrol's parent organization is a nonprofit organization called Red Light Resources International, which works to support survivors of human trafficking. Parasol Patrol also offers support for starting local chapters in other states.

Player vs. Hunger

https://playervshunger.org

Player versus Hunger is an organization that works to collect donations in support of food pantries throughout the U.S. Gamers and streamers play to fund raise for the organization which then donates to food banks and pantries.

Pop Culture Classroom

https://popcultureclassroom.org/

Pop Culture Classroom (PCC) is a nonprofit organization based in Denver, Colorado, that works to increase literacy, build community, and celebrate diversity. PCC is the official charity partner of Fan Expo Denver and works to provide professional development for educators at the convention and year-round.

Pop Culture Hero Coalition

https://www.popculturehero.org/

The Pop Culture Hero Coalition is a nonprofit organization that works to fight bullying and promote social emotional learning in schools. Founded in 2013, this organization often partners with genre celebrities and was cofounded by Chase Masterson from *Star Trek: Deep Space Nine*.

Random Acts

https://www.randomacts.org/

Random Acts is a U.S.-based nonprofit organization (501c3) founded in 2010 by actor Misha Collins. Volunteers perform random acts of kindness and donate their money and time in support of various causes. Random Acts also sustains two ongoing projects: a free high school in Nicaragua and a children's center in Haiti. Random Acts has 145 volunteers in 26 countries. Volunteers can apply to open positions anytime, anywhere. There are also regional representative positions that help connect individuals to volunteer opportunities in specific areas. Random Acts also offers the capability for people to submit their ideas and apply for funding to Perform an Act of Kindness.

StackUp

https://stackup.org

Stack Up is a nonprofit organization that looks to support veterans by connecting veterans and civilians through a shared love of video games. From supplying video game care packages to deployed service members to staffing a suicide prevention/mental health support hotline, there are many opportunities to help.

Stands

https://shopstands.com/

Stands is an online retailer of fandom-related merchandise. Stands partners with celebrities to promote designs featuring fan artists in time-limited campaigns. A portion of sales from campaigns is donated to charity. Charities supported by current and past campaigns include: Random Acts, New Leash on Life, and a variety of charities supporting stroke awareness, food security, and people facing breast cancer.

FANDOM-SPECIFIC ORGANIZATIONS

BTS
One In An ARMY

https://www.oneinanarmy.org/

One In An ARMY is a global collective of BTS fans who volunteer their time toward various campaigns and missions. They are not officially affiliated in any way with BTS or Big Hit Entertainment.

CRITICAL ROLE
Critical Role Foundation
https://critrole.com/foundation/

The Critical Role Foundation is a nonprofit organization founded by stars of the *D&D* web series *Critical Role*. The foundation partners with other charities, including 826LA, the First Nations Native Youth and Culture Fund, and Shanti Bhavan, a school for low-income children in India.

FIREFLY
Can't Stop the Serenity
https://www.cantstoptheserenity.com/

Can't Stop the Serenity (CSTS) is a fan-led organization that hosts screenings of the film *Serenity* to raise money for the gender rights organization Equality Now. In addition to hosting these screenings, CSTS also organizes other types of fundraisers and has an online store that donates its proceeds.

STAR TREK
The Federation
https://trekfederation.com/

The Federation is a nonprofit organization that uses *Star Trek* as a gateway into community service and volunteerism. Created by Gene Roddenberry and Russ Haslage in 1984, the Federation does everything from donating money to support the people of Ukraine to organizing volunteers in the aftermath of tornadoes and other natural disasters.

#StarTrekUnitedGives
https://www.startrek.com/startrekunitedgives

Star Trek United Gives is an annual social media donation event where Paramount+ donates a dollar for each tweet using the hashtag. Donations are split between charities that support LGBTQIA+ equality, veterans, and humanitarian aid.

STAR WARS
The 501st Legion

https://www.501st.com/

The 501st Legion is an organization of volunteer costume enthusiasts. Volunteers attend events in costume and raise money for charities, including the Make-A-Wish Foundation.

The Rebel Legion

https://rebellegion.com/

The Rebel Legion also features *Star Wars* costume enthusiasts and volunteers—this time from the Rebel Alliance side of things. Volunteers attend events in costume and raise money for charity. The Rebel Legion also sponsors "Rebels For A Cause," a weeklong charity event held annually.

SUPERNATURAL
SPN Survivors

https://spnsurvivors.org/

SPN Survivors is a nonprofit organization that works to promote mental health and prevent suicide. Volunteers with SPN Survivors provide programming in schools, increase awareness and offer support at fan conventions, and raise money for charity.

XENA: WARRIOR PRINCESS
Australian Xena Information Page

https://charity.ausxip.com/

The Australian Xena Information Page (AUSXIP) hosts an annual online auction of Xena-related merchandise. The proceeds benefit the Starship Foundation (which supports children's health) and the House of Bards (a nonprofit theater company).

Xenite Retreat

https://www.xeniteretreat.com/

The Xenite Retreat is best described as an adult summer camp for fans of *Xena: Warrior Princess*. Although it's an event, it's included here as a resource because attendees have raised over $50,000 for various charities in just five events! Retreat attendees have supported numerous charities, including summer camp opportunities for inner-city kids, support for families affected by pediatric cancer, and support for youth arts programs.

GOVERNMENT AND LEGAL INFORMATION RESOURCES

American Civil Liberties Union

https://www.aclu.org/know-your-rights/protesters-rights

The American Civil Liberties Union (ACLU) is a nonpartisan, public-interest law firm that works to safeguard civil liberties, including the right to free speech.

Combined Federal Campaign

https://www.opm.gov/combined-federal-campaign/

The official website for the US-based Combined Federal Campaign—an initiative to help partner workplace giving with charitable organizations—is helpful for information on whether or not your employer may match donations.

Fandom and the Law: A Guide to Fan Fiction, Art, Film & Cosplay by
Marc H. Greenberg

Law professor Marc Greenberg's analysis of fan fiction, art, film,
and cosplay also includes useful information about how US legal
doctrines and copyright law affect fan-creator relationships.

National Center for Transgender Equality

https://transequality.org/about

The National Center for Transgender Equality is a US-based
organization founded by transgender activists that advocates for
policy and social changes for the betterment of the lives of transgender people.

National Council of Nonprofits

https://www.councilofnonprofits.org/tools-resources/how-start-nonprofit

The National Council of Nonprofits is a US nonprofit organization dedicated to supporting nonprofit organizations nation-
wide. The site listed here is a great resource for those interested
in starting their own nonprofit. Your state or city may also have
details about starting a nonprofit organization on their official
websites. In the United States, these sites typically end in .gov.

Physicians for Human Rights

https://phr.org/our-work/resources/preparing-for-protecting-against-and-treating-tear-gas-and
-other-chemical-irritant-exposure-a-protesters-guide/

Physicians for Human Rights is an organization that works to
document and investigate human rights violations.

Southern Poverty Law Center

https://www.splcenter.org/about

The Southern Poverty Law Center (SPLC) is an anti-racist legal
organization that primarily operates in the southern United States.

Transgender Law Center

https://transgenderlawcenter.org/

The Transgender Law Center is a trans-led nonprofit organization that employs a number of strategies to improve the lives and rights of transgender people, including legal assistance in some cases.

The US Congress

https://www.congress.gov/

The official website of the US Congress includes a searchable database of current and past federal legislative information.

MEDIA SOURCES

British Broadcasting Corporation (BBC)

The BBC is a UK-based, tax-funded media network including news, radio, and television channels.

National Public Radio (NPR)

https://www.npr.org/

NPR is a US-based nonprofit public radio network with local affiliates that provide news, podcasts, and music.

Public Broadcasting Service (PBS)

https://www.pbs.org/

PBS is a US-based nonprofit television network.

PETITION RESOURCES

Care2

https://www.care2.com/

Care2 is a social networking site that seeks to connect activists with one another, with other organizations, and with other institutions. Users can create a profile, as well as sign and share petitions. Care2 is also a for-profit company, and users agree to the use of their data by the website.

Change.org

https://www.change.org/

Change.org is an online site that enables users to easily create and share petitions. Change.org is very easy to use, but it is a for-profit company; donations made through the platform do not go directly to the petition organizers.

REFERENCES

Anderson, Benedict. *Imagined Communities: Reflections on the Origin and Spread of Nationalism*. London and New York: Verso, 2016.

Balisger, Philip. "Making Political Consumers: The Tactical Action Repertoire of a Campaign for Clean Clothes." *Social Movement Studies* 9, no. 3 (July 2010): 311–29. doi:10.1080/14742 837.2010.493672.

Benford, Robert D., and David A. Snow. "Framing Processes and Social Movements: An Overview and Assessment." *Annual Review of Sociology* 26 (2000): 611–39. doi:10.1146/annurev. soc.26.1.611.

Brough, Melissa M., and Shangita Shresthova. "Fandom meets activism: Rethinking civic and political participation." *Transformative Works and Cultures* 10 (2012): 1–27. doi:10.10.3983/twc.2012.0303.

Coe, Anna-Britt, Isabel Goicolea, Anna-Karin Hurtig, and Miguel San Sebastian. "Understanding How Young People Do Activism: Youth Strategies on Sexual Health in Ecuador and Peru." *Youth & Society* 47, no. 1 (October 2012): 3–28. doi:10.1177/0044118X12464640.

Collins, Misha. "Even Without a Home, We Always Had a Family Meal." *New York Times*, April 15, 2020. https://www.nytimes.com/2020/04/15/parenting/misha-collins-supernatural-family-meal.html.

Collins, Randall. "Social Movements and the Focus of Emotional Attention." In *Passionate Politics: Emotions and Social Movements*, edited by Jeff Goodwin, James M. Jasper, and Francesca Polletta, 27–44. University of Chicago Press, 2001.

Cook, Tanya. "The Resistance Is Geeky." *Medium*, January 2, 2018. https://aknerdfighting.medium.com/the-resistance-is-geeky-106b907a655b.

Copeland, Carolyn. "Performers are using their craft as a vehicle for activism." *Prism Reports*, November 2, 2020. https://www.dailykos.com/stories/2020/11/2/1991016/-Performers-are-using-their-craft-as-a-vehicle-for-activism?fbclid=IwAR0im2YCrwPPVEyLQcML2QGeQHp2UTp4EQ2NAC6iH7zbjCi57avXwKv0Fqk.

Corning, Alexandra F., and Daniel J. Myers. "Individual Orientation Toward Engagement in Social Action." *Political Psychology* 23, no. 4 (December 2002): 703–29. doi:10.1111/0162-895X.00304.

Corrigall-Brown, Catherine. "We Are Not All Activists: The Development and Consequences of Identity." In *Patterns of Protest: Trajectories of Participation in Social Movements*. Stanford University Press, 2011.

Craddock, Emma. "Doing 'enough' of the 'right' thing: the gendered dimension of the 'ideal activist' identity and its negative emotional consequences." *Social Movement Studies* 18, no. 2 (2019): 137–53. doi:10.1080/14742837.2018.1555457.

Durkheim, Émile. *The Elementary Forms of the Religious Life.* Translated by Karen E. Fields. New York: Free Press, 1995.

Earl, Jennifer, and Katrina Kimport. "Movement Societies and Digital Protest: Fan Activism and Other Nonpolitical Protest Online." *Sociological Theory* 27, no. 3 (September 2009): 220–43. doi.10.1111/j.1467-9558.2009.01346.x.

Ellis, Emma Grey. "*Handmaids Tale* Garb Is the Viral Protest Uniform of 2019." *Wired*, June 5, 2019. https://www.wired.com/story/handmaids-tale-protest-garb/.

Gamson, William A., and David S. Meyer. "Framing Political Opportunity." In *Comparative Perspectives on Social Movements: Political Opportunities, Mobilizing Structures, and Cultural Framings*, edited by Doug McAdam, John D. McCarthy, and Mayer N. Zald, 275–90. Cambridge University Press, 1996.

Golus, Carrie. "Squishy Hugs: Why is Misha Collins, AB'97, the object of so much affection?" *The Core: College Magazine of the University of Chicago*, 2017. http://thecore.uchicago.edu/Winter2017/features/squishy-hugs.shtml.

Granovetter, Mark S. "The Strength of Weak Ties." *American Journal of Sociology* 78, no. 6 (May 1973): 1360–80. doi:10.1086/225469.

Hamann, Emily. "'Supernatural' star lends aid to help end homelessness for Bellingham families." *Bellingham Business Journal*, January 3, 2018. https://bbjtoday.com/blog/supernatural-star-lends-aid-to-help-end-homelessness-for-bellingham-families/35592/.

Hansen, Claire. "Young Voters Turned Out in Historic Numbers, Early Estimates Show." *US News & World Report*, November 7, 2018. https://www.usnews.com/news/politics/articles/2018-11-07/young-voters-turned-out-in-historic-numbers-early-estimates-show.

Huddy, Leonie. "From Group Identity to Political Cohesion and Commitment." In *The Oxford Handbook of Political Psychology*, edited by Leonie Huddy, David O. Sears, and Jack S. Levy, 737–73. Oxford University Press, 2013.

Jasper, James M. *The Art of Moral Protest: Culture, Biography, and Creativity in Social Movements*. University of Chicago Press, 1997.

Jasper, James M. "Emotions and Social Movements: Twenty Years of Theory and Research." *Annual Review of Sociology* 37 (August 2011): 285–303. doi:10.1146/annurev-soc-081309 -150015.

Jenkins, Henry. "'Cultural Acupuncture': Fan Activism and the Harry Potter Alliance." *Transformative Works and Cultures* 10 (2012). doi:10.3983/twc.2012.0305.

Jenkins, Henry. "'Decreasing World Suck': Fan Communities, Mechanisms of Translation, and Participatory Politics." *Confessions of an Aca-Fan* (blog). June 25, 2013. http:// henryjenkins.org/blog/2013/06/decreasing-world-suck-fan -communities-mechanisms-of-translation-and-participatory -politics.html.

Jenkins, Henry. *Textual Poachers: Television Fans and Participatory Culture*. New York and London: Routledge, 2013.

Jenkins, Henry, Sangita Shresthova, Liana Gamber-Thompson, Neta Kliger-Vilenchik, and Arely Zimmerman. *By Any Media Necessary: The New Youth Activism*. New York University Press, 2016.

Klandermans, Bert. "Transient Identities? Membership Patterns in the Dutch Peace Movement." In *New Social Movements: From Ideology to Identity*, edited by Enrique Laraña, Hank Johnston, and Joseph R. Gusfield, 168–84. Philadelphia: Temple University Press, 1994.

Klandermans, P. G. "Identity Politics and Politicized Identities: Identity Processes and the Dynamics of Protest." *Political*

Psychology 35, no. 1 (February 2014): 1–22. doi.10.1111/
pops.12167.

Klar, Malte, and Tim Kasser. "Some Benefits of Being an Activist:
Measuring Activism and Its Role in Psychological Well-
Being." *Political Psychology* 30, no. 5 (September 2009): 755–77.
doi.10.1111/j.1467-9221.2009.00724.x.

Kligler-Vilenchik, Neta, Joshua McVeigh-Schultz, Christine
Weitbrecht, and Chris Tokuhama. "Experiencing Fan Activism:
Understanding the Power of Fan Activist Organizations
Through Members' Narratives." *Transformative Works and
Cultures* 10 (2012). doi.10.3983/twc.2012.0322.

Larsen, Katherine, and Lynn S. Zubernis. *Fangasm: Supernatural
Fangirls*. University of Iowa Press, 2013.

Mason, Jessica. "Interview: How *Supernatural*'s Misha Collins'
Gish Scavenger Hunt Changes Lives." *The Mary Sue*, August 9,
2018. https://www.themarysue.com/misha-collins-gish
-interview/.

Melucci, Alberto. "The process of collective identity." In *Social
Movements and Culture*, edited by Hank Johnston and Bert
Klandermans, 41–63. University of Minnesota Press, 1995.

Miley, Amber. "Stop Pretending we are all Nice People: The Dark
Side of Being a K-pop Fan," *The Kraze*, June 27, 2020. https://
thekrazemag.com/latest-updates/2020/6/27/stop-pretending
-we-are-all-nice-people-the-dark-side-of-being-a-k-pop-fan
?rq=bullying.

Passy, Florence. "Socialization, Connection, and the Structure/
Agency Gap: A Specification of the Impact of Networks
on Participation in Social Movements." *Mobilization: An
International Quarterly* 6, no. 2 (2001): 173–92. doi.10.17813/
maiq.6.2.v6u4wg67x87w943h.

Polletta, Francesca, and James M. Jasper. "Collective Identity and Social Movements." *Annual Review of Sociology* 27 (2001): 283–305.

Putnam, Robert D. *Bowling Alone: The Collapse and Revival of American Community*. New York: Simon and Schuster, 2000.

Smelser, Neil J. *Theory of Collective Behavior*. London: Collier-MacMillan, 1962.

Snow, David A., and Robert D. Benford. "Clarifying the Relationship Between Framing and Ideology." *Mobilization* 5, no. 1 (2000): 55–60.

Snow, David A., and Robert D. Benford. "Ideology, Frame Resonance, and Participant Mobilization." *International Social Movement Research* 1 (1988): 197–217.

Stein, Louisa Ellen. *Millennial Fandom: Television Audiences in the Transmedia Age*. University of Iowa Press, 2015.

Stryker, Sheldon, Timothy J. Owens, and Robert W. White, eds. *Self, Identity, and Social Movements*. University of Minnesota Press, 2000.

Stuart, Avelie, Emma F. Thomas, Ngaire Donaghue, and Adam Russell. "'We may be pirates, but we are not protesters': Identity in the Sea Shepherd Conservation Society." *Political Psychology* 34, no. 5 (2013): 753–77. doi.10.1111/pops.12016.

Tarrow, Sidney. "Mentalities, Political Cultures, and Collective Action Frames: Constructing Meanings Through Action." In *Frontiers in Social Movement Theory*, edited by Aldon D. Morris and Carol McClurg Mueller, 174–202. Yale University Press, 1992.

Taylor, Verta, and Nancy E. Whittier. "Collective Identity in Social Movement Communities: Lesbian Feminist Mobilization." In *Frontiers in Social Movement Theory*, edited by Aldon D. Morris and Carol McClurg Mueller, 104–130. Yale University Press, 1992.

Terriquez, Veronica. "Training Young Activists: Grassroots Organizing and Youths' Civic and Political Trajectories." *Sociological Perspectives* 58, no. 2 (2015): 223–42. doi.10.1177/0731121414556473.

Thomas, Emma F., Craig McGarty, and Kenneth I. Mavor. "Aligning Identities, Emotions, and Beliefs to Create Commitment to Sustainable Social and Political Action." *Personality and Social Psychology Review* 13, no. 3 (2009): 194–218. doi.10.1177/1088868309341563.

van Zoonen, Liesbet. "Imagining the Fan Democracy." *European Journal of Communication* 19, no. 1 (March 2004): 39–52. doi.10.1177/0267323104040693.

Vlogbrothers. "How to Be a Nerdfighter: A Vlogbrothers FAQ." YouTube video. December 27, 2009. https://www.youtube.com /watch?v=FyQi79aYfxU.

Young Democrats of America. 2019 Fall National Committee Meeting Resolutions. PDF document. December 8, 2019. https://www.yda.org/sites/default/files/Copy%20of%20 BHM%20Resoultions%20Committee.pdf.

Zubernis, Lynn S., ed. *Family Don't End with Blood: Cast and Fans on How Supernatural Has Changed Lives*. Smart Pop, 2017.

Zubernis, Lynn S., ed. *There'll Be Peace When You Are Done: Actors and Fans Celebrate the Legacy of Supernatural*. Smart Pop, 2020.

Zubernis, Lynn S., and Katherine Larsen. *Fandom at the Crossroads: Celebration, Shame and Fan/Producer Relationships*. Cambridge Scholars Publishing, 2012.

ACKNOWLEDGMENTS

We would like to, first and foremost, thank you, the fans. Without you, this book would not exist. It is you who have educated and inspired us, every step of our journey, from idea to publication. We especially would like to thank everyone who agreed to be interviewed in the process of researching this book. Specifically, we would like to thank fellow fan Lynn Zubernis, who gave us a platform to write about the power of fandom for good in her book, *There'll Be Peace When You Are Done*, through which we found our amazing and supportive publisher, Smart Pop. As a publisher, Smart Pop has been a perfect home for this book. Thank you to everyone at Smart Pop for believing in this project and for guiding us to publication. Thank you to the amazing Rachel Miner for sharing her time and talents with us. It means the world to have one of the most generous and insightful people we know not only notice our work but invest energy in supporting it!

Tanya would like to thank her family—Levi, Dean, Maria, and Perrin—thank you for everything, always. You are the reason I keep fighting. I would also like to thank everyone who helped me with this project including: Riley Santangelo, Allison, Anita, Anita M., Ashley R., Jamie, Bex, Crisha, Michi, Anna, Sasha, Sarah, Maggie & the Utah Browncoats, Jules, Nicole, Katie, Karla, Jeremy, Jill, Francine, Darcy, Jen L.G., Alana King (and her awesome dad who helped us get to the tacos—very important!), Brandy, Sherrill, Brian, Candace, Victoria, Tasha, Penny C. and the entire Xenite Community, Melody, Spencer, Brit, Kevin, Bonnie, Leisa, Jen, Julie, Pasha, Eli, Paige, Jess, Liza, Sarah G., Hansi (Squee Media), Christine, Charli, Princess, Colleen (Nerd Alert News), Charlie, Michelle H., Kristin L., Lara, Jan, Maggie, Zoe, January, Melissa, Cindy, E, Kai, Lynn, and anyone I unintentionally missed. Research conducted for this book was generously funded by the American Council of Learned Societies' Mellon/ACLS Community College Fellowship Award. Thank you to Dr. Jennifer Dale and Dr. Betsy Oudenhoven (president emerita) with the Community College of Aurora for helping me earn this fellowship and their support of my work. And thanks to Misha Collins for sharing an early abstract of this project on social media, even if his main goal was to troll Jared Padalecki. Thankful that it helped Kaela find me because they are the best.

Kaela would like to thank their chosen family, Megan Davis and Sam Wirth. You have always listened to my fannish musings with love and enthusiasm, even when I have insisted on discussing shows you do not watch. You have been a constant source of support in all things, including this book, and I love you both. Kaela would also like to thank two of their mentors, Drs. Peter Goldblum and Elizabeth (Beth) Fassig. Peter, I have learned so much from your guidance about program development and your own work with marginalized communities. Your mentorship helped drive my career in ways I never expected, ways that inevitably led me to this book. Beth, you were one of the first people to encourage me to celebrate my involvement in fandom and activ-ism as part of my identity as a psychologist. It is because of you that I had the confidence to reach out to Tanya at the start of this project. I thought of your words, "I want to know who *you* are as a psychologist" often, while writing this book. This is who I am as a psychologist. Lastly, I would like to thank several members of my fandom family, who have engaged in fandom acts of kindness with me over the years—Alysa, Bill, Maddy, Stephanie, Brandy, Marta, Sagan, Elana, Paul, Stacie, Randi, Lauren, Bunny, Pasha, Eli, Kate, Shannon, Larisa, and Lizzie. You were all a huge piece of my heart while writing this book.

ABOUT THE AUTHORS

Tanya Cook

Tanya Cook is a sociology professor at the Community College of Aurora. Cook earned a bachelor's degree, master's degree, and PhD, all in sociology, from the University of Wisconsin-Madison. After participating in the Greatest International Scavenger Hunt (GISH) for the first time in 2014, Cook became fascinated with fans who do charity work and activism. Since 2016, Cook has worked with Kaela Joseph to research fandom as a social movement. Cook and Joseph have contributed chapters to Lynn Zubernis's book *There'll Be Peace When You Are Done: Actors and Fans Celebrate the Legacy of Supernatural* and to April Vian, Melissa Kennedy, and Shani Irvine's book, *CONventional Wisdom: Every Con Has a Story.* In 2019, Cook was one of twenty-six community college faculty awarded a research grant from Mellon/ACLS to support sociological research on fandom. Cook received an inclusive excellence teaching award from her college in 2018 and works as a peer mentor on diversity and inclusion efforts. Cook also writes academic articles and presents at both professional and comic conventions about popular culture, pedagogy, and disability. Her 2022 article on COVID-19 and invisible disability won the Barbara R. Walters Award from the Eastern Sociological Society. When she's not trying to find new ways to use popular culture and fandom to democratize the classroom, you can probably find her at Comic-Con. Cook lives in Colorado with her family.

Kaela Joseph

Kaela Joseph is a licensed clinical psychologist living and working in the San Francisco Bay Area as a program manager, clinic director, and clinical supervisor. Kaela earned a bachelor's degree in psychology and sociology from the University of Colorado Boulder and a PhD in clinical psychology, with an emphasis in LGBTQ psychology, from Palo Alto University. Kaela has published and presented at professional conferences and Comic-Cons on the topic of fan activism, as well as on fandoms and sexuality. Works by Kaela in these areas can be found in Lynn Zubernis's book *There'll Be Peace When You Are Done: Actors and Fans Celebrate the Legacy of Supernatural* and in April Vian, Melissa Kennedy, and Shani Irvine's book, *CONventional Wisdom: Every Con Has a Story.* Kaela also regularly presents on health care equity, systems improvement, and gender-diverse care at professional conferences, as well as in health care settings to clinicians and clinical trainees. Kaela has additionally published in academic journals on the topic of lived experience of mental health challenges among mental health care providers. Kaela attributes much of their own identity development as an activist, as well as their coming out as queer and nonbinary, to participation in fandoms, including many years of taking part in the Greatest International Scavenger Hunt (GISH), which benefits the nonprofit Random Acts and other causes.